KEYSTONE

TOMBSTONES

Volume One

Joe Farrell and Joe Farley

Cover image: *Columbia Cemetery* by Lawrence Knorr

Keystone Tombstones: Volume One

SECOND SUNBURY PRESS EDITION

Printed in the United States of America
October 2012

ISBN 978-1-934597-67-5

Published by:
Sunbury Press, Inc.
50-A West Main Street
Mechanicsburg, PA   17055

www.sunburypress.com

Mechanicsburg, Pennsylvania   USA

And, when he shall die,
Take him and cut him out in little stars,
And he will make the face of Heaven so fine
That all the world will be in love with night
And pay no worship to the garish sun.

William Shakespeare

Acknowledgments

From the very beginning of our adventure, we have received help and support from almost everyone we have told about this project. We are grateful for the genuine interest and enthusiasm that made us determined to complete this volume and plan for additional volumes.

Over the last year, we have spent many hours traipsing through cemeteries all over Pennsylvania in all kinds of weather. Cemeteries, we have learned, are very confusing places, even with maps, so we are particularly grateful to Richard Sauers of Ivy Hill Cemetery in Philadelphia who helped us through the maze that is Ivy Hill and first exposed us to the term "grave goods", meaning the mementos left by visitors at graves. He saved us hours and was very encouraging and offered some names for us to consider.

Kathleen Lukaszewiez of Chartiers Cemetery was also extremely helpful. She drove us to the graves we had an interest in and offered personal stories relative to her meetings with Myron Cope. In addition, she contributed names and ideas for our consideration.

Ralph (Red) Ellmaker, Joe Keener, and Christopher McNally all contributed ideas and names for our consideration that were used in the project as did Bill Isler, Joe Quattorcchi and that walking lexicon of PA history, Burke McLemore. Jeff Briel was also helpful and supportive of the idea and assisted in finding a publisher for our book.

We also offer our heartfelt thank you to the Vietnam Veterans of Mechanicsburg for their efforts to preserve The Lincoln Colored Cemetery and preventing it from fading into oblivion and to the 9th Pennsylvania Reserves, a Civil War reenactment unit in Pittsburgh area for their establishment of the Civil War and WWI Headstone Restoration Project at Chartiers Cemetery. You can learn how to donate to restore the headstone of 120 Civil War and 5 WWI veterans at www.9thpareserves.org.

Sharon Farley's typing and editorial comments allowed us to complete the project in a timely manner. The editing talents of young Jim Farley were invaluable in the production process. We are aware that Jim provided assistance while he was working on an Eagle Scout project and doing work on AP courses he plans to take his senior year. We thank him for finding the time to assist us.

We also thank Jesse Hereda for his assistance in establishing our company, Idle Minds, Inc.

Finally we offer our gratitude to our publisher, Larry Knorr, for his personal interest in this book and his guidance and advice throughout the process and to Allyson Gard, our editor, who sat patiently and listened while we defended and rationalized each and every mistake.

Contents

Introduction by Joe Farley

On May 21, 2010, I retired after working for the Commonwealth of Pennsylvania for 35 years. For a majority of those years, my boss was a man by the name of Joe Farrell. One of the agencies we worked together for was the Pennsylvania Public Utility Commission. Joe and I shared a lot over those years. We played on the same softball team, we were partners in a fantasy football league, I watched his kids grow up, and he saw mine from the time they were born. We did numerous after work Friday happy hours together, and at the same time proved to be a productive work team (much to the chagrin of the majority of utilities in Pennsylvania). In short, we had become pretty good friends.

After I retired, the question I kept getting asked was "What will you do now?" While I didn't know the precise answer, I knew that whatever it was I would like it better than working. For goodness sakes I'm Irish, I knew there had to be something better to do on my own. Well as luck or fate would have it, Farrell had just published a book titled "Confessions of a Catholic Schoolboy: Jesus Runs Away and Other Stories". I found that book to be a very hilarious and fun read about the Catholic Education system that both Joe and I had experienced. The two of us began talking about writing a book together.

Our first idea was to travel the length of the Lincoln Highway (Route 30) all the way through Pennsylvania. We felt we could chronicle the trip and take photos of interesting attractions and sights. When I mentioned this idea to my wife, I think it's safe to say that Mrs. Farley wasn't very keen on the project. For some reason, she believed that the combination of the two Joes and the Lincoln Highway could only result in trouble. In addition, she mentioned the idea at a meeting of her book club and a few of the members said that a book similar to what we were proposing had already been written. The latter point really didn't deter us as we felt whatever we would write would be different than any previous books on the subject. There was, however, at least for me, no way around my wife's initial objection.

During this time, my oldest son Corrigan was home on summer break from the University of Pittsburgh. Corrigan started as a computer science major, but after taking a philosophy course or two, he decided to major in that as well. One day, he asked me if I had any old philosophy books. I told him I didn't know but I'd check. I did find a couple during my search and I also came upon a book I had purchased way back in 1982. This book was titled "To Absent Friends" written by the sportswriter Red Smith. I began to reread the book which is a collection of Smith's columns about his friends in the sports world who had recently passed away. As I read I began thinking about the famous (and infamous) people who were buried in

Pennsylvania and the possibility of writing a book about them.

I set up a meeting with Joe Farrell at Nick's Café in downtown New Cumberland. Joe and I often met at Nick's to have a few drinks and play their trivia game. When he arrived, I explained my idea and we began to discuss it. Soon, in addition to writing about famous people buried in the Commonwealth, we had decided we would visit their graves and photograph the sites. In addition, we decided to photograph any other tributes that would add to their stories. At the conclusion of the meeting, we agreed to bounce the idea off friends and relatives to see if other people thought the project to be worthwhile.

Of course the first person I went to was my wife, and she thought it was a great idea. To what extent the fact that there are no bars in graveyards influenced her I can only guess. She later told me that the members of her book club also thought it was a great idea. As a matter of fact, Farrell and I received no negative feedback from anybody we talked to. We met again (at Nick's) and decided we would do the research, visit the graves , and write this book.

The first thing we needed to do was put together a list of the famous people we would visit and identify the cemeteries in which they were laid to rest. Joe Farrell promptly produced an initial list of 77 names. He had identified famous politicians, business leaders, statesmen, sports figures, entertainers, writers, military heroes, and gangsters. With this list in hand, we began making visits.

Every visit was planned in advance. We identified the graves we would visit, the location of the cemetery, and to the best of our ability the location of the individual gravesites. One of the things we decided we would do was visit every Medal of Honor recipient we could locate. While we realized that it would not be possible to devote a chapter to all these heroes, we decided we could identify where they were buried. This goal was one of the factors that led to the "If You Go" sections you will find at the end of each chapter in this book. In those sections, we identify other graves you might want to visit, local establishments where we stopped for refreshments, and other attractions in the area you might find interesting. No business mentioned in these sections provided us with any compensation. As a matter of fact, we didn't inform any of them that they would be included in this volume.

We learned early on in our travels that cemeteries are laid out without any easily understood pattern. Even armed with section and plot numbers, we were having difficulties locating gravesites because of the randomness of the layouts. For example, you can be standing in section A of a graveyard and section B might be located hundreds of yards away with sections D, T, K, M, and W lying between them. In addition, in many cemeteries we found the sections to be poorly marked and in some cases not marked at all. As a result, we began going directly to the cemetery office to obtain maps and directions to the sites we hoped to visit. The other thing we noticed was that some cemeteries were very well kept while others seemed neglected. All of the photographs in this book show the gravesites as we found them. We would urge local communities to pay attention to maintaining these historic sites.

There were other factors impacting our project as we began writing up the chapters. We were discovering other famous people who were buried in the state but were not on our original list. It became obvious to us that we were not going to be able to cover everybody in a single book. We had a meeting with a potential publisher (who would become the actual publisher) and he suggested two volumes one covering eastern and the other western Pennsylvania. We initially planned to go with that idea but later had to change plans because there was a large difference in the number of gravesites we had identified between the east and the west. So, we decided to go with multiple volumes, but abandoned the idea of a geographical split.

In terms of the actual writing we split up the chapters between us. Upon completion of a chapter, we would share it with the other author who would review it, identify mistakes, and suggest changes or additions. One of the things we both agree on is that writing this book was an educational experience for us. We learned all kinds of things about the people covered in this volume. In some cases, we were writing about people we never even heard of, or knew little about, and ended up totally surprised by the accomplishments of those individuals.

As mentioned previously, we will be following this up with subsequent volumes. We have a long list of people buried in Pennsylvania that we have yet to cover. Some of the people mentioned in the "If You Go" sections of this book may be fully discussed in a future volume. We had a great time putting this initial volume together and hope that you have a great time reading it and possibly visiting some of the "Keystone Tombstones" identified in the following pages.

Willie Anderson with his arm around Alex Smith

1.
"Golf's Forgotten Legend"

William (Willie) Law Anderson
County: Philadelphia
Town: Philadelphia
Cemetery: Ivy Hill Cemetery
Address: 1201 Easton Road Philadelphia, PA

Only four golfers have won four United States Open championships. Three of the four, Bobby Jones, Ben Hogan, and Jack Nicklaus are well known to golf fans everywhere. Such is not the case for the first man to do it. Not only did William (Willie) Law Anderson win four Opens, he did something the other three never accomplished, Anderson won three in a row.

Anderson was born on October 21, 1879, in Scotland. He became a licensed caddie at the age of eleven. In addition, he apprenticed as a golf club maker under Alex Aitken. Aitken's clubs, by the year 1896, were being exported to the United States and he had also produced a set of clubs for the British Prime Minister. Anderson would later use the skills he learned from Aitken in designing some of his own clubs

In 1896, Anderson, his father, and his brother Tom arrived in the United States. The following year, Anderson entered the United States Open for the first time. He was tied for the lead with Joe Lloyd when they reached the final hole. Lloyd's approach shot stopped eight feet from the pin. He sank the putt for a birdie three, beating Anderson by one stroke.

By now Anderson was making his living as a golf professional. He worked at ten different clubs over a fourteen year period. During this time he also competed in tournaments and exhibitions. His first big tournament win came in 1899 at the Southern California Open. He won the by one stroke, beating Alex Smith, a man who would finish second to him twice in United States Open play.

In 1901, the Open was played near Boston, Massachusetts at the Myopia Hunt Golf Club. After 72 holes Anderson and Smith, were tied at 331. The tournament ended on a Friday, but the first 18 hole playoff in Open history did not take place until Monday. Saturday and Sunday were club member days, so the course was unavailable. That Monday, Anderson won his first Open, beating Smith once again by a single stroke.

In 1902, Anderson entered the Western Open. At the time winning the Western was comparable to winning the Masters today. Anderson won the tournament by recording a 299 over the 72 holes. In one round he shot a 69. The win made Anderson the first player to hold two major American golf titles. In addition, with his score of 299, he became the first golfer to score under 300 in a 72 hole tournament held in America. That same year he again competed in the United States Open where he finished fifth.

The 1903 Open was held at Baltusrol in New Jersey. Anderson had worked at this club as its first professional in 1898. After 36 holes, Anderson had a six stroke lead. The margin evaporated nine holes later when he carded an 8. At the conclusion of the 72 hole tournament he found himself in a tie with Davie Brown. The playoff took place in a driving rain and Anderson prevailed by two strokes. His Open streak began.

In 1904, Anderson became the first two time winner of the Western Open. He won the tournament by beating Alex Smith by four strokes. The win earned him $200.

A week later, he was once again playing in the United States Open. This one was played at the Glen View Course in Chicago. In 1904, there would be no playoff. Anderson set a scoring record by posting a 303. He won easily by five strokes. He was now a three time Open champion and he had won two in a row.

The following year the Open started out poorly for Anderson. In the first round, he shot an 81 and he followed that with an 80. After 36 holes, he was five strokes off the lead and a third straight Open title looked out of reach. In round three, Anderson started strong. After the fourth hole, he was two under for the day. He continued to narrow the margin between himself and the leaders until he took the lead. By the 70th hole, he found himself four shots in front. He held on to win by two. He was now a four time Open champion, and he had won three in a row.

Anderson would never win another Open title, though he would be quite competitive. After his fourth win he finished third once, fourth twice, fifth twice, eleventh twice, and fifteenth once. His days of winning tournaments were not behind him. He won the Western Open in both 1908 and 1909, thus becoming the first four time winner of that event.

By this time Anderson's health had begun to deteriorate. He was unable to defend his Western Open title in 1910. Anderson played in his last tournament in July of 1910 at the Deal Golf and Country Club in New Jersey. While his game was clearly not what it once was, he finished just out of the money in 12th place.

Anderson continued playing exhibitions where he made most of his money. In October of 1910, he traveled to Pittsburgh to play a series of matches with other pros and amateurs. The final match he played was lost on the last hole. He returned to his home in Philadelphia on October the 24th. The next day he died. He was 31 years old.

How good was he? His contemporaries had no problem comparing him to Bobby Jones and Walter Hagen. He was known for his accuracy, whatever club was in his hand. In addition, pressure did not bother him. He was viewed by his competitors as a formidable foe that would make you crack before he would. One would have to conclude he was among the greatest golfers of his time and perhaps the greatest in America in the early 1900's.

The cause of his death remains a controversy. It was reported that he died from arteriosclerosis, a fatal hardening of the arteries. One newspaper said it was a brain tumor. The official report named the cause of death as epilepsy. One golf historian reported that Anderson had drank himself to death.

Anderson was inducted into the golf Hall of Fame in 1975. The great Gene Sarazen accepted the honor on his behalf. He had finally joined his special fraternity.

Anderson is buried in the Ivy Hill Cemetery in Philadelphia. His tombstone, which is unique, was erected by the Eastern Professional Golfers Association. In the opinion of the authors it is worth seeing. In fact, if you visit you might want to leave a golf ball or tee at the grave.

If You Go:

Others buried in Ivy Hill Cemetery include Franklin Gowen and Bill Tilden. Gowen was famous for leading the prosecution, some would say persecution, of the Molly Maguires in the 1870's (See Chapter 21). Tilden was a tennis great who dominated that sport in the 1920's and 30's (see Chapter 27). Both Harold Melvin of Harold Melvin and the Blue Notes and Marion Williams the famed gospel singer are also buried at Ivy Hill, but they are in unmarked graves. You can still visit their gravesites as the folks working in the cemetery office will be glad to provide you with their locations. In addition if you are at Ivy Hill, you are about a mile away from Holy Sepulcher Cemetery. Frank Rizzo and Connie Mack are buried there. Rizzo was a colorful and controversial Mayor of Philadelphia (See Chapter 25). Mack was a legendary major league baseball manager (See Chapter 16).

Here lies a golfer who can be compared to the all-time greats. Names like Jones, Hogan, and Nicklaus leap to mind.

James Buchanan (1791-1868), 15th President of the USA

2.
"Pennsylvania's Only President"

James Buchanan
County: Lancaster
Town: Lancaster
Cemetery: Woodward Hill Cemetery
Address: Bounded by Strawberry, South Queen, and Chesapeake Streets.

James Buchanan was the fifteenth President of the United States. He was the only President never to marry and the only President from Pennsylvania. Perhaps he was the only President from Pennsylvania because he is regarded as one of the worst ever to hold the office. It could be that his performance in office has adversely affected the chances of other Pennsylvanians that have aspired to hold the highest office in the land.

We looked at fifteen different polls, including Schlesinger, Chicago Tribune, Siena College, C-Span, Wall Street Journal, and others. In each poll, he was ranked in the bottom Quartile and five times he was rated the worst President. The best he was rated was in a 1982 poll, where he was fourth from last (36th). In 2006 and in 2009, a survey of presidential historians organized by the University of Louisville listed Buchanan's feeble actions to oppose efforts by Southern states to secede from the Union as the worst blunder by any president.

Buchanan was born on April 23, 1791, in Cove Gap, Pennsylvania. He attended Dickinson College in Carlisle, Pennsylvania. At one point, he was expelled from the school for behavior issues. Given a second chance, he graduated with honors in 1809. After graduation, he relocated to Lancaster where he studied law. He was admitted to the Pennsylvania bar in 1812. Even though he was strongly opposed to the War of 1812, Buchanan volunteered to fight and served in the defense of the city of Baltimore.

His political career began in 1814, when he was elected to the Pennsylvania House of Representatives as a member of the Federalist party. He served five terms in the United States House of Representatives from March 4, 1821 – March 4, 1831. He did not seek re-election in 1830 and from 1832 to 1834, served as Ambassador to Russia.

In 1834, he won a special election to the United States Senate, was re-elected twice, and resigned in 1845. President Polk offered Buchanan a nomination to the US Supreme Court after the death of Supreme Court Justice Henry Baldwin in 1844, but he declined the nomination. The seat was then filled by Robert Cooper Grier. Buchanan then served as Secretary of State under President Polk from 1845 to 1849. He received this appointment in spite of the fact that Polk's Vice President George Dallas opposed his selection. While serving as Secretary of State, he aided in the negotiations that resulted in the Oregon Treaty of 1846. This treaty established the 49th parallel as the northern boundary of the western United States. No Secretary of State has ever become President since Buchanan.

Here lies Pennsylvania's only President.

When Franklin Pierce became President, Buchanan was appointed to serve as Minister to the United Kingdom. While serving in this capacity (1853-1856) he helped draft the Ostend Manifesto. This document described the rationale for the United States to purchase Cuba from Spain and implied that the US would declare war if Spain refused. The rationale was that Cuba should be acquired as a slave state. Once published, the idea was denounced in both the Northern States and Europe. The Manifesto was a major blunder for the Pierce administration and greatly damaged efforts to annex Cuba.

Buchanan sought the Democratic Presidential nomination in 1844, 1848, and 1852 but was unsuccessful each time. Finally, in 1856, he was nominated on the seventeenth ballot largely due to the fact that he was in England during the Kansas-Nebraska debate and did not have to take a position on the expansion of slavery. He went on to defeat John Freemont, the first Republican Party candidate for President, in the election.

Buchanan took over the presidency well aware of the growing divisions in the country between the north and the south over slavery. His strategy to address the problem was to maintain a sectional balance in his appointments and to allow the Supreme Court to make the decision relative to the expansion or restriction of slavery in the territories.

Two days after Buchanan took office, the Supreme Court issued the Dred Scott decision. The decision was written by Chief Justice Taney and it held that Congress had no constitutional authority to restrict the spread of slavery in the territories. It was widely believed that Buchanan supported the decision. The Dred Scott decision was hailed in the south and denounced throughout the north. Abraham Lincoln called Buchanan an accomplice of slave power. There is little doubt that on a personal level, Buchanan favored slaveholders' rights. He believed that the slaves were treated with kindness by their masters. He was a northern man who favored the policies of the south. He once vetoed a bill passed by Congress to create more colleges for he believed the "there were already too many educated people". He believed that the Southern States could not secede from the Union and did little to prevent it.

By and large, most of Buchanan's policies drove a wedge between northern and southern Democrats; he was weakening his own party. As a result, in the 1858 elections, the Republicans took control of the House of Representatives. Once they had control of the House, the Republicans used their power to block anything Buchanan wanted done. This included the purchase of Cuba. His motivation in this pursuit remained the expansion of slavery. It's ironic to note that had Buchanan succeeded in that purchase, the Spanish American War may have been avoided.

When Buchanan delivered his inaugural address he said he would only serve one term. True to his word he did not seek re-election in 1860. The Democratic party was so divided by this time that when they held their convention no candidate was able to secure the votes needed to become the presidential nominee. With the convention deadlocked the southern wing walked out and nominated Vice President John C. Breckinridge for the presidency. The remainder of the party nominated Stephen Douglas as their candidate. When the Republicans met they nominated Abraham Lincoln who, with the democrats split, was sure to be elected.

The Commanding General of the Army, Winfield Scott, warned Buchanan that Lincoln's election would result in the secession of a number of southern states. He urged the president to send more federal troops and supplies to these areas to protect federal property. Buchanan ignored Scott and took no action which allowed the southern states to secede without having to deal with federal interference.

When he left office on March 4, 1861, he told President-elect Lincoln that he hoped the new President was as happy entering the Executive Mansion as he was to be leaving. He retired in great wealth to his home Wheatland in Lancaster, PA. He died at his home on June 1, 1868 at the age of 77. He is buried in Woodward Hill Cemetery in Lancaster.

Just across the road from President Buchanan lies Frederick Muhlenberg America's first Speaker of the House of Representatives.

If You Go:

James Buchanan's home called "Wheatland" is also in Lancaster. Visitors can tour the residence. We visited Wheatland but didn't have time to take the tour. The grounds and the exterior of the residence, however, are beautifully maintained, so if you are in the area you may want to take advantage of the tour. While there are many signs around the area directing people to Wheatland that is not the case with the grave. We had to ask the staff of Wheatland for directions to the cemetery and apparently many people do since they had them ready in print to give us. The grave is the best maintained in an old decaying cemetery.

Across from Buchanan's grave, facing his gravestone just a few yards away, is the grave of Lt. L.E. Bostwick who was killed at the Battle of Antietam on September 17, 1862. The stone says that he was 25 years old and that Antietam was his 19th battle. We found it interesting that the tombstone of such a young man who had died in the Civil War was facing the grave of the President who did so little to prevent it.

Also buried within yards of Buchanan is Frederick Muhlenberg. Mr. Muhlenberg was a delegate from Pennsylvania to the Continental Congress, served in the Pennsylvania State legislature, and was head of the State's convention that ratified the U.S. Constitution in 1787. He became one of Pennsylvania's first congressmen and was the very first Speaker of the House of Representatives in U.S. history. His grave is badly deteriorated but marked with a plaque.

John Andrew Shulze who served as Pennsylvania's Governor from 1823 to 1829 is buried here as well.

Pearl S. Buck

3.
"The Good Earth"

Pearl Buck
County: Bucks
Town: Perkasie
Cemetery: Green Hills Farm Grounds
Address: Off Route 313 West follow signs to Pearl
Buck Homestead

Pearl Buck won the Nobel Prize for Literature in 1938. She was the first woman to be awarded this honor. Her novel, "The Good Earth", was the best- selling fiction book in the United States in both 1931 and 1932. In 1932, it was named a Pulitzer Prize winner.

She was born Pearl Sydensticker, on June 26, 1892, in Hillsboro West Virginia. Buck's parents were missionaries. As a result, she grew up in China. As a matter of fact, she learned how to speak Chinese before she was able to speak English. When she was 19, she left China to attend Randolph-Macon Women's College in Virginia. There, she studied psychology.

She graduated Phi Betta Kappa in 1914. That same year, she returned to China as a Presbyterian missionary. In 1917, she married John Lossing Buck, another missionary, who specialized in agriculture. Immediately after the wedding, the couple moved to Nanhsuchou in the very rural Anhwei province. The community was very poor and it was here that Buck began gathering information she would use in writing "The Good Earth" and many other stories involving China.

In 1920, the Bucks moved to Nanking, where they both had obtained teaching positions at a local university. The couple's first child, a daughter who they named Carol, was born that same year. The child was profoundly retarded. In addition, because a uterine tumor was discovered during delivery, Buck had a hysterectomy. The bad luck continued as Buck's mother died in 1921.

The Bucks returned to the United States in 1924. During this period Buck earned a Masters degree from Cornell University. The following year they adopted a daughter who they named Janice. In the fall of 1925, they returned to China.

In 1927, a battle known as the "Nanking Incident" began. It involved forces under Chiang Kai-shek, those supporting the communists, and

Here lies Pearl Buck returned to the good earth in a beautiful grave on the property where she did most of her writing.

Chinese warlords. Several westerners were killed. Buck and her family, including her father, hid in a hut with a poor Chinese family. They spent a terrifying day in hiding before being rescued by American gunboats. Later, the Bucks moved back to Nanking for a short time. However, because of the dangers that remained, they left China for good in 1934.

Buck's marriage, though it lasted for 18 years, was never a happy one. In 1935, she and her husband divorced. Through her writing, Buck had met John Walsh who was a publisher for the John Day Company. This company published her first novel, "East Wind, West Wind", as well as "The Good Earth." In 1935, after her divorce became final, she married Mr. Walsh.

By this time, Buck had bought a farmhouse, known as Green Hills Farm, in Bucks County, Pennsylvania. It was here she and her second husband lived. Over the course of time, they adopted six more children. The farm itself is now on the Registry of Historic Buildings and approximately fifteen thousand people visit each year.

Back in the states, Buck became active in many causes, including civil rights and women's rights. In 1942, she and her husband created the East West Association. Its purpose was to encourage a cultural exchange between Asia and the West. She was angered that adoption services of her time considered Asian and mixed race children to be unadoptable, so in 1949, she founded Welcome House. It was the first agency whose aim was to promote inter-racial adoption.

During the Chinese Cultural Revolution, Buck was described as an "American Cultural Imperialist." This was used to deny her entrance to China when President Nixon visited there in 1972.

Pearl Buck died of lung cancer on March 6, 1973. She was eighty. She is buried on the grounds of Green Hills Farm. Her grave site is easy to find as it sits to the left as you enter the property. She picked a beautiful and peaceful area in which to be laid to rest. Buck designed her own tombstone with Chinese characters that represent the name Pearl Sydensticker.

If You Go:

Green Hills farm in Perkasie is a beautiful place and it is open to the public. You can tour Buck's house and see where she did, not only her writing, but her work on the causes she adopted. Her grave is unique and very well maintained. In addition, as you drive through Perkasie, you will notice numerous shops and restaurants that you might want to visit.

John Burns

4.
"The Hero of Gettysburg"

John Burns
County: Adams
Town: Gettysburg
Cemetery: Evergreen Cemetery
Address: 99 Baltimore Street

On July 1, 1863, soldiers of the 7th Wisconsin Infantry and the 24th Michigan Infantry were stunned to see an elderly man dressed in dark trousers and a blue swallowtail coat with brass buttons and a high black silk hat join them in McPherson's Woods to await an attack by Confederate troops. He fought beside these men of the famous Iron Brigade throughout the afternoon, in one case shooting a charging Confederate officer from his horse.

His name was John Burns. Burns was born on September 5, 1793, in Burlington, New Jersey. He was a veteran of the War of 1812 where he served as an enlisted man and fought in numerous battles. In 1846, when war broke out with Mexico, Burns was one of the first to volunteer. He also served with valor in that conflict. When the Civil War began, he was 67 years old, but he immediately volunteered to serve in the union army. He was rejected due to his advanced age. Though rejected for combat duty, he was permitted to serve the army as a teamster. However, within a short time, he was sent home to Gettysburg. Little did he realize, at the time, that this would give him the opportunity to fight.

Confederates rode into Gettysburg on June 26. During General Jubal Early's brief occupation of Gettysburg, Burns was the local constable. The rebels had him jailed for his adamant resistance and assertion of civil authority. As Confederate troops were leaving for Harrisburg, he was released from jail and he promptly arrested some of the Confederate stragglers. He held them in custody until the arrival of Federal Calvary under Brigadier General John Buford on June 30.

The next day, when major combat erupted, Burns calmly took up his flintlock musket and simply walked out to the scene of the fighting. On his way he encountered a wounded Union soldier and asked if he could borrow his more modern rifle for the battle. The soldier agreed and Burns moved on, putting cartridges in his pockets. He ran into Major Thomas Chamberlin of the 150th Pennsylvania Infantry and asked to be allowed to fight with the

This monument sits on the Gettysburg battlefield near where Burns took his spot beside Union troops.

The gravesite of a man who wasn't about to let the rebels enter his town without a fight.

regiment. Chamberlin referred him to the Regimental Commander Colonel Langehorne Wister who agreed to let him fight. Burns was wounded three times and when the Union forces fell back under Confederate pressure, the Union soldiers were forced to leave him behind. Although wounded and exhausted, he was able to crawl away from his rifle and bury his ammunition so that when captured by confederates, he could claim he was a noncombatant. He succeeded in convincing the Confederates of such and his wounds in the arm, leg, and breast were treated by their surgeons. Had Burns not convinced his captors, he would have been subject to summary execution as a non-uniformed combatant.

After the battle, Burns became a national hero. Matthew Brady's photographer Timothy O'Sullivan snapped a picture of Burns recuperating from his wounds and took the story back home to Washington. The inventor of baseball, Major Abner Doubleday, called Burns, "the Hero of Gettysburg." When President Lincoln came to Gettysburg a few months later to dedicate the Soldiers National Cemetery, it was John Burns he wanted to meet. President Lincoln and Burns walked together from David Will's house to the Presbyterian Church on Baltimore Street. Lincoln extended his personal thanks to John Burns on their walk. His fame spread all across the Nation and in 1864, the famous poet Bret Harte published a poem about Burn's exploits called "John Burns of Gettysburg" and Congress passed a special act granting him a pension.

In the last few years of his life, Burns suffered from dementia. He would often wander from his home. He somehow found his way to New York City where on a winter's night in December 1871, he was discovered in a state of destitution. He was sent home to Gettysburg where he died of pneumonia on February 4, 1872. He was 78 years old.

A monument depicting a defiant Burns carrying his rifle and with a clenched fist can be found on McPherson's Ridge near where Burns fought with the Iron Brigade. The monument was dedicated on July 1, 1903, the 40th anniversary of the battle. Burns is buried in historic Evergreen Cemetery in Gettysburg. His grave is one of only two graves there with permission to fly the American flag twenty-four hours a day. The other grave is Ginnie Wade (see chapter...). A full length biography titled "John Burns: the Hero of Gettysburg" by Timothy H. Smith was published in 2000.

The tombstone of Charles Collis a Medal of Honor recipient for his actions during the battle of Fredericksburg. The men who served under him erected this monument.

Amos Humiston is the only enlisted man to have his own monument on the Gettysburg battlefield.

If You Go:

Gettysburg is a fantastic town steeped in history. There is so much to see and do that we can only scratch the surface here. In the historic Evergreen Cemetery are many interesting graves including those of Ginnie Wade (see chapter 28) and Hall of Fame baseball player Eddie Plank. Nearby Gettysburg National Cemetery is perhaps the most hallowed ground in our country and a sight to behold. It is the site of Lincoln's famous Gettysburg Address and the graves of 3512 Union soldiers of which 979 are unknown.

Among those buried there are:

Amos Humiston who is the only enlisted man at Gettysburg who has his own monument on the battlefield. Humiston was killed on July 1, 1863 the first day of the battle. When his body was discovered later that week, he was holding an ambrotype (an early kind of photograph) of three small children. There was nothing else to identify him and the few soldiers from his unit, Company C, 154th New York Volunteer Infantry, who survived had moved on before he was found. Efforts to discover his identity using the picture started with a story in the Philadelphia Inquirer with the headline "Whose Father is He?" The story swept the North and his widow saw the photograph in a magazine and realized that her devoted husband was dead. The family was living in Portville, New York and Amos had been dead for four months. The outpouring of sympathy was so great that the proceeds from fund raising allowed for the creation of an orphanage in Gettysburg for children of soldiers. Amos Humiston is buried in the New York Section of the National Cemetery and his monument is on Stratton Street between York Street and the railroad, beside the fire station. A book titled "Gettysburg's Unknown Soldier: The Life, Death, and Celebrity of Amos Humiston" by Mark H. Dunkleman was published in 1999.

Cyrus James is also buried in the New York plot. He is believed to be the first soldier killed in this famous and monumental battle. He was killed by Ewell's forces in a skirmish north of town before the main engagement.

Charles Henry Tucky Collis was awarded the Congressional Medal of Honor for his bravery at the Battle of Fredericksburg on December 13, 1862. He survived war and has an impressive grave in the National Cemetery.

William E. Miller was awarded the Congressional Medal of Honor for his bravery on the third day of the Battle of Gettysburg. He is buried in the Officer's Section in the National Cemetery.

George Nixon was wounded during the second day of the Battle of Gettysburg. That night, as he lay on the battlefield between Union and Confederate lines he cried out in pain. Musician Richard Enderlin crawled out and dragged Private Nixon most of the way back to safety then dashed the rest of the way with Nixon in tow. For this act, Enderlin was promoted to Sergeant and awarded the Medal of Honor. Nixon's wounds were mortal and he died in a hospital seven days later. He was the great-grandfather of Richard Nixon, our 37th president. His grave is in the Ohio plot.

5.
"Pennsylvania's Political Kingmaker"

Simon Cameron
County: Dauphin
Town: Harrisburg
Cemetery: Harrisburg Cemetery
Address: 521 North 13th Street

To some, Simon Cameron was a brilliant Pennsylvania politician who built a political machine to advance his friends and himself. Others view him as one of the most corrupt public servants in the history of the Commonwealth. One thing that is certain is that he was one of the most influential Pennsylvanians of his time. Indeed one could argue if not for a man like Simon Cameron, Abraham Lincoln may never have been elected president.

Cameron was born on March 8, 1799, in Maytown, Pennsylvania. Because his parents were poor, he received very little formal education. Cameron's parents both died by the time he was nine, leaving him an orphan. Even as a youth he was driven and ambitious. He became an apprentice to a printer who was the editor of the Northumberland Gazette in order to ready himself to enter the field of journalism. By the time he was 21, his hard work began paying off as he found himself editor of the Bucks County Messenger.

Cameron then secured a position with the printing firm of Gales and Seaton. This firm happened to be the publishers of the Congressional debates. He made the most of this opportunity by making political friends in Washington and learning the art of politics. In 1824, he returned to Harrisburg, married Margaret Brua, and purchased a local newspaper. As the editor of his own paper he issued strong editorials addressing the issues of his day. His influence grew and in 1825 he was made state printer for the Commonwealth of Pennsylvania. Within a year he was also appointed to the position of adjutant general as part of the governor's staff.

One thing we know for sure about Cameron is that the man could identify opportunities. He saw all the internal improvement going on in Pennsylvania and surrounding states. He jumped in, constructing both railroads and canals. To aid in financing these ventures he founded a bank. This was in keeping with what he did his whole life: mixing private business with politics.

Simon Cameron

Cameron was a strong supporter of Democrats during the administrations of both Andrew Jackson and Martin Van Buren. During this time, he also helped elect James Buchanan to the United States Senate. President Van Buren rewarded Cameron in 1833 by appointing him commissioner in charge of settling Winnebago Indian claims. His term here was tainted by scandal and ultimately led to his dismissal. It seems that Cameron felt it would be a good idea to adjust the claims on notes paid through his own bank. While his political career suffered damage, his ambitions remained and he still was confident in the methods that he had made the choice to employ.

In 1845, Cameron put together a coalition consisting of some Democrats, Whigs, and members of the Native American party and succeeded in his quest to be elected to the United States Senate. He served one term.

When the Republican party began to form Cameron saw, yet again, opportunity. He built up a political machine that returned him to the Senate in 1858 as a Republican. After that election, he attempted to position himself to be the party's nominee for president in 1860.

The Republican convention was held in Chicago, and Cameron arrived with little support outside Pennsylvania. However, the shrewd politician knew he had bargaining power. It was accepted that whoever the eventual nominee was, he was going to need Pennsylvania's support to secure the nomination and head the ticket. On the first ballot, William Seward received 173 and ½ votes. Lincoln was second with 102 votes and the other candidates were far back. It would take 233 votes to secure the nomination.

Lincoln had chosen David Davis, who was a long time friend, to represent him at the convention. He gave Davis the explicit instruction not to make deals that would bind him in any way. However, after the initial ballot, Davis was convinced that he needed Cameron's Pennsylvania votes to stop Seward. In order to secure Pennsylvania's support, Davis promised Cameron a cabinet position. Lincoln had received a mere 4 votes from Pennsylvania on the initial ballot but that number increased to 44 on the second. Honest Abe had seized the momentum and on the third ballot he won the nomination.

Lincoln was not happy about the deal that had been made with Cameron. As a matter of fact he made no effort to contact the Pennsylvanian. That did not deter Cameron. He made the trip to Springfield, Illinois to meet with the president-elect. Cameron left this meeting with a letter from Lincoln that promised he would be named either the Secretary of the Treasury or the Secretary of War. Later Lincoln, faced with opposition to the Cameron appointment, attempted to recall the letter. Not only did Cameron not respond to Lincoln's request, he persuaded elements of the

Pennsylvania Legislature to pressure Lincoln on his behalf. Finally, Lincoln nominated Cameron to the position of Secretary of War. He did so because he felt Cameron could do less damage there than in the Treasury Department.

Then came the Civil War and the role of the War Department grew in terms of importance. It did not take long for rumors of corruption in the department begin to grow. When the war began Lincoln made clear to the members of his cabinet that the emancipation of the slaves, at this point was not an option. Cameron and some Republican legislators were urging Lincoln to recruit Negro soldiers. Lincoln agreed to use Negroes as laborers in the army but not as soldiers. It was Lincoln's view that arming Negroes would lose the support of southerners still loyal to the union.

Cameron went his own way on the issue. He released his annual report in 1861 and it publicly contradicted the president by taking the position that the Negroes should be freed and be made part of a Negro Army. When word of this report reached Lincoln (Cameron had not run it past the president), he ordered it be withdrawn and rewritten. It turned out to be too late as both versions found their way to the press. The publication of the two reports showed an administration at war against not only the rebels, but against themselves.

During the holiday season between 1861 and 1862 things came to a head. Complaints about irregularities in the War Department had begun to flood Congress. On two occasions Congress demanded that Cameron provide information on contracts awarded since he assumed office. He ignored both requests. In response, the House set up a committee to investigate the War Department. The investigation produced a 1,109 page report that was damning to the administration. Cameron and his "agents" were accused of ignoring the competitive bidding process. It claimed that the department had supplied the army by buying from favored suppliers who were often dishonest. The report alleged that the War Department purchased huge amounts of tainted pork, rotten blankets, knapsacks that couldn't hold up in foul weather, and hundreds of diseased and dying horses at inflated prices. The report also claimed that the department sold condemned Hall carbines cheaply, bought them back for $15.00 apiece, turned around and sold them again for $3.50, and then bought them back at the price of $22.00 a piece.

By early in 1862, Lincoln concluded that Cameron had to go. The president made it easy on him. On January 11, 1862, the president wrote to Cameron, noting that he had requested a change in position. The president said he was pleased to inform Cameron that he was going to nominate him to be minister to Russia. One wonders what Abe may have done had Siberia been an option.

Cameron served in Russia a very short time before returning to Pennsylvania. He regained his Senate seat in 1867 and held it until 1877, when he was sure his son would replace him. Cameron then retired to his farm in the Maytown area where he died on June 26, 1889. He was 90 years old. Perhaps he summed up his public career best when he said, "An honest politician is one who, when he is bought, will stay bought." Simon Cameron is buried in the Harrisburg Cemetery.

Final resting place of one of Pennsylvania's most controversial politicians.

If You Go:

Also buried in the Harrisburg Cemetery are John Geary (See Chapter 9) and Vance McCormick (See Chapter 18). In addition, the authors urge you to stop at the cemetery office where you can pick up a booklet that provides for a walking tour of the premises. It's a very old and interesting cemetery that includes a section where both union and confederate casualties of the Civil war were laid to rest. You are also very close to the State Capitol building which is worth seeing and where tours are offered. If you choose to dine in Harrisburg the city offers a restaurant row on 2nd street that provides multiple options. The authors would point out that within about a half mile of the cemetery there is a small Italian place called the Subway Cafe. It is located on Herr Street about a half a block below Cameron Street. The Subway offers fishbowls of beer and great pizza.

The Four Horsemen of Notre Dame - Don Miller, Elmer Layden, Jim Crowley and Harry Stuhldreher

6.
"Half the Horsemen"

James (Jim) Crowley and Harry Stuhldreher
Counties: Lackawanna and Allegheny
Towns: Moscow and Pittsburgh
Cemeteries: Saint Catherine's and Calvary
Addresses: Route 435 and Main Street, Moscow
718 Hazelwood Avenue, Pittsburgh

On October 18, 1924, the famed sportswriter Grantland Rice was covering the Notre Dame - Army football game. After Notre Dame's 13-7 win, Rice authored what may well be the most famous sports story lead off ever written. It began,

"Outlined against a blue-grey October sky, the Four Horsemen rode again. In dramatic lore their names are Death, Destruction, Pestilence, and Famine. But those are Aliases. Their real names are Stuhldreher, Crowley, Miller, and Layden. They formed the crest of a South Bend cyclone before which another fighting Army team was swept over the precipice at the Polo Grounds this afternoon as 55,000 spectators peered down upon the bewildering panorama spread out upon the green plain below."

With Rice's inspiration, a Notre Dame student publicity aide named George Strickland, made sure the name stuck. When the Irish team arrived back in South Bend he placed the four players, dressed in their uniforms and each holding a football, on four horses he obtained from a local stable. The famous photograph was quickly picked up by the wire services, and the legend of the Four Horseman of Notre Dame became forever embedded in the hearts and minds of American sports fans.

The horsemen were put together by the legendary coach Knute Rockne. They are widely considered to be the greatest college football backfield in the history of the game. They appeared in 30 games together and won all but two. Both losses were at Nebraska. In 1922, the Cornhuskers prevailed 14-6. They followed that with a 14-7 win in 1923. Playing at Notre Dame in 1924, the horsemen sought their revenge and succeeded, winning 34-6. They remain the only college backfield where all four members were voted into the College Football Hall of Fame. Two of the four, Jim Crowley and Harry Stuhldreher are buried in Pennsylvania.

Jim Crowley was born on September 10, 1902, in Chicago, Illinois. Shortly after his birth his family moved to Wisconsin. He picked up football by playing at Green Bay East High School. He was coached at the time by a man named Curly Lambeau. Lambeau would go on to found the Green Bay Packers.

Crowley graduated from high school and in 1921 enrolled at the University of Notre Dame. He went out for and made the football team. Coach Rockne, known as "The Rock", nicknamed him "Sleepy Jim" because of his droopy eyelids and his laid back demeanor. This latter trait I would come to witness 48 years later. Rockne saw he had some talented young players and he decided to make a backfield out of them. Though none of the four were taller than six feet or weighed more than 162 pounds, the Rock placed Crowley at left halfback, Don Miller at right halfback, Elmer Layden at fullback, and in charge of it all, Stuhldreher at quarterback.

Notre Dame contended for the national title in Football in both 1922 and 1923. In both years, however, losing to Nebraska ended those hopes. In 1924 there was no way of denying the Irish the title. Only two teams, Army and Northwestern, came within a touchdown of beating Notre Dame. In addition, Rockne decided that Notre Dame would play in the Rose Bowl against a powerful Stanford squad. Stanford was coached by the legendary Pop Warner and was also undefeated, though they did have one tie. The Stanford team was led by the great Ernie Nevers at quarterback and they dominated the game offensively if one looks at the statistics. However, the statistic that mattered most, the final score, was 27-10 in Notre Dame's favor. The Irish intercepted 5 Stanford passes, and returned 2 for touchdowns. Layden (who returned both interceptions for scores) and Crowley both made outstanding plays in the Irish victory. Notre Dame was declared the National Champion. The game marked Notre Dame's first appearance in a bowl game. They would not play in another until 1969.

The year 1924 proved to be Crowley's best at Notre Dame. He led the team in rushing yards and in scoring. He was also named to the All American team along with his teammates Layden and Stuhldreher.

After graduation, Crowley had a short professional football career, playing in just three games for the Green Bay Packers and the Providence Steamrollers. In 1925, he made his last appearance as a player when he took the field for the Waterbury Blues. He was joined in the backfield by his former teammate and fellow horseman Harry Stuhldreher. The Blues won the game 34-0 and Crowley scored three touchdowns. Following the contest, he picked up his check and left the team.

While his playing days were behind him, Crowley was not done with football. First, he became an assistant coach at the University of Georgia. In 1929 Michigan State hired him to be their head coach. His head coaching debut proved successful as he led Michigan State to a record of 22-8-3 in four seasons.

At the time, Fordham University was a college football powerhouse. In 1933, Crowley left Michigan State to coach Fordham. His success continued. He turned Fordham into one of the top defensive teams in the country. In 1936, he made future Notre Dame coach Frank Leahy his defensive line coach. Crowley and Leahy developed a line that would become famous. The line earned its own nickname, the "Seven Blocks of Granite." One of the blocks was none other than Vince Lombardi, who would go on to have considerable success coaching in the National Football League.

In 1939, a Crowley coached Fordham team appeared in the first televised football game. In that game, Fordham easily defeated the Waynesburg Yellow jackets by a score of 34-7. Crowley's last game at Fordham was in the 1942 Sugar Bowl. His team defeated Missouri 2-0. Crowley left Fordham after compiling a record of 56-13-7.

In 1946, a new professional football league, the All-American League, was established. Crowley became its first commissioner. Crowley resigned that position after one year to become part owner and head coach of the worst team in the league, the Chicago Rockets. His pro coaching career was a short and unsuccessful one. In 1947, his team went 1-13 and he hung it up as a coach prior to the 1948 season.

With his football career over Crowley moved to Pennsylvania to become an insurance salesman. In 1953, he relocated to Scranton, Pennsylvania to become station manager and sports director of an independent television station. In 1955 he was named chairman of the Pennsylvania State Athletic Commission. He remained as chairman until 1963.

Crowley was inducted into the College Football Hall of Fame in 1966. At the time, he was making a living as an after dinner speaker at various banquets. In 1969 he was the speaker at my high school team's basketball dinner. Here he demonstrated how Rockne came to nickname him "Sleepy Jim." While his stories were very humorous his expression and the tone of his voice never changed. In addition, the droopy eyelids were ever present and perhaps even more pronounced than they were when he was a younger man. I do recall him saying that there was one problem with being a member of the four horseman. He said whatever you did after that didn't matter. You were always one of the horsemen. He swore that he could have been governor of a state and that he would still be introduced as one of the four horsemen.

Jim Crowley was the last surviving horseman. He died in Scranton on January 15, 1986. He was 83 years old. He is buried in a very modest grave in Saint Catherine's Cemetery in Moscow, Pennsylvania.

Harry Stuhldreher was born on October 14, 1901 in Massillon, Ohio. It was here he spent his formative years. At the time Massillon fielded a professional football team. The star of the team was none other than a man by the name of Knute Rockne. There are stories that Stuhldreher would carry Knute's gear for him as a way to get into the games.

Stuhldreher's family moved to Pennsylvania where he played football for and graduated from the Kiski School in the town of Saltsburg. After graduation, he decided to attend the University of Notre Dame. There are those who believe this decision may have been influenced by his earlier interactions with Rockne.

Whether the gear carrying stories are true or not is open to speculation. One thing that isn't is that Rockne identified Stuhldreher as the man who would lead what became the most famous offense in college football history. He was very small for a football player standing at 5 feet 7 inches and weighing all of 151 pounds. His contemporaries described him as cocky and ambitious. Rockne saw him as a leader.

As detailed earlier, the four horsemen experienced tremendous success at Notre Dame. We already covered the 1925 Rose Bowl where the Irish bested Stanford. What is not well known is that early in that game, Stuhldreher broke his ankle. He refused to leave the game. In spite of the injury, he played a key part in the Irish win.

Stuhldreher later told stories about that 1924 Notre Dame team. He said that at one point, Rockne was concerned that the Horsemen were getting all the credit for the wins and that the line (now known as the seven mules) was a second thought. According to Stuhldreher, Rockne called the team together for a vote. "Which is more important to this team," he asked, "the line or the backfield?" According to Stuhldreher the line won by a vote of 7 to 4.

Very much like Crowley and his fellow horsemen, Stuhldreher went into coaching after his college playing days were over. His first job was at Villanova University. He was head coach there for 10 years starting in 1925, and he compiled a record of 65-25-9. Based on this success, he was hired by the University of Wisconsin as both head football coach and athletic director.

His tenure at Wisconsin had its ups and downs. While he coached the Badgers to be the Big Ten runner-up twice, there were unsuccessful seasons mixed in. At the time, as they do today, Wisconsin fans took their football seriously. During a bad year, the local newspaper printed a letter to the editor. The writer said, "We have a great offensive coach at one of our high schools and a great defensive coach at the other. What we need to do is fire Stuhldreher and hire these two guys as co-coaches." That evening when Stuhldreher arrived home from work, his oldest son was waiting for him newspaper in hand. He was angry. He demanded to know if his father had read the letter. Stuhldreher admitted he had, and, trying to calm his son down, basically said that you have to expect these things when it's not going well. His son responded, perhaps in jest, "Heck those two guys are bums. *My* coach is the guy that should have your job."

Stuhldreher wrote two books. One was called "Knute Rockne, Man Builder." The book was used as a source for the movie "Knute Rockne All American" that starred Pat O'Brien and Ronald Reagan. The film gave Reagan his nickname, the "Gipper."

Stuhldreher left Wisconsin for Pittsburgh to join U. S. Steel in 1950. In 1958, he was inducted into the College Football Hall of Fame. On January 26, 1965, he died in Pittsburgh of acute pancreatitis. He was 63. He is buried in a modest grave in Calvary Cemetery in Pittsburgh Pennsylvania.

The Four Horsemen remain a major part of the tradition that is Notre Dame Football to this very day. The Notre Dame bookstore continues to market shirts, sweats, cups, and glasses that show the famous photo of the horsemen atop their steeds. Every year, the students and alumni of the university sponsor a game day shirt. These same students, and many others, wear this shirt to every home game. The 2011 shirt has the picture of the Four Horsemen on the front. In light of all that the horsemen have contributed to Notre Dame, we were surprised at how simple and modest their grave sites remain. In Stuhldreher's case, we had to visit the cemetery office twice to get directions before we could find it. On our second trip, the office worker told us that Stuhldreher was under memorialized. We agree and note that there are Notre Dame clubs all over the Commonwealth. In our opinion, perhaps a couple of these clubs should take on the task of finding a way to honor these two horsemen in an appropriate manner.

Perhaps no one summed up the horsemen better than the legendary sportswriter Red Smith. Ironically, Smith was a friend and protégé of Grantland Rice. After Stuhldreher's death, Smith acknowledged all that the four had accomplished after leaving Notre Dame. Then he put it all together. He wrote, "Yet it was as a unit, and as undergraduates, they made their greatest contributions. They gave the game something special and precious that can't be coached and can't be manufactured. People call it romance."

If You Go:
Should you choose to visit Jim Crowley at Saint Catherine's, there are a couple of other graves you may want to visit. Former Pennsylvania Governor Bob Casey is buried there and so is Patrick DeLacy who was awarded a Congressional Medal of Honor. You are also in the vicinity of two other cemeteries covered in this volume (See Chapter 7 on Congressman

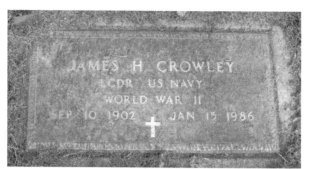

Here lies Sleepy Jim Crowley, one of the Four Horsemen of Notre Dame, in a very modest grave.

Dan Flood and Chapter 13 on Mary Jo Kopechne). In addition, the area has many other attractions including quality golf courses, a triple A minor league baseball team, a major concert venue, and more than a few fine dining establishments. We recommend a visit to Woodlands Inn and Conference Center. The Woodlands offers multiple bars and eating establishments. The rooms are reasonably priced. You may also want to look into their vacation packages.

Should you visit Harry Stuhldreher at Calvary Cemetery you can find a number of gravesites worth seeing. Frank Gorshin (See Chapter 10), the actor best known for his role as the "Riddler" on the Batman TV series is buried here. Another actor, Gene Lyons, who is best remembered for playing Commissioner Dennis Randall, on the show "Ironsides" is interned here. So is David Lawrence (See Chapter 14), former Mayor of Pittsburgh and Governor of Pennsylvania. The Hall of Fame boxer Harry "The Human Windmill" Greb, is here as well. Speaking of boxers the light heavyweight champion from 1939-1941, Pittsburgh's own Billy Conn, was also laid to rest here. Of course there is plenty to do in Pittsburgh. There is a first rate amusement park known as Kennywood and the city also has a fine zoo. When we made our trip, we took in a Pirates game. They have a beautiful ballpark and we had a great time.

Very modest gravesite of the quarterback of the legendary Four Horsemen of Notre Dame.

7.
"Dapper Dan"

Congressman Dan Flood
County: Luzerne
Town: Wilkes Barre
Cemetery: St. Mary's Cemetery
Address: 695 N. Main Street

Daniel Flood was born in Hazleton, Pennsylvania in 1903. He attended schools in Wilkes-Barre, a city where he would become a hero in later years. He earned a law degree from the Dickinson School of Law in Carlisle, Pennsylvania and began practicing law back in Wilkes-Barre in 1930.

Flood fancied himself an actor and, in fact, did appear on stage in local theatre productions and on various vaudeville stages. Some believe that his dabbling in acting was the foundation for his political style. He was nothing if not flamboyant, with a waxed moustache that curled up at both ends and a preference for all white suits sometimes complete with a cape. In addition, his speaking style drew comparisons to Shakespearean actors.

This author, who lived in the Congressman's district in the 1970's, heard him speak on two very different occasions. The first time took place in 1972 at Bloomsburg State College where he was the keynote speaker at a mock Democratic Convention. Congressman Flood was clearly annoyed by the reception he received (he was ignored by virtually all present). He had only begun his speech when he began waving his arms as he shouted into the microphone "I'm a United States Congressman and I deserve respect." This statement resulted in a combination of boos and laughter and the Congressman quickly cut his speech short and left the podium. This author heard him again in 1977 at a Friendly Sons of Saint Patrick's dinner in Hazleton. As you might imagine the reception was far different. Flood arrived at the dinner wearing one of his many white suits (with a green tie of course) and the crowd erupted in applause as he took his place at the main table. He gave a rousing speech about all the great things the Irish had done in America that was interrupted numerous times by applause. At its conclusion he left the hall to a standing ovation.

Flood was first elected to Congress in 1944 but he was defeated in '46. He won again in 1948, but lost the seat in the huge republican sweep in 1952. He regained the 11th district seat in 1954 and after that was reelected 12 consecutive times, often without any real opposition. From 1954 on,

President Kennedy (left) with Congressman Daniel "Dan" Flood on the steps of the White House.

Flood amassed the power that made him a mover and a shaker in Washington.

House Speaker Sam Rayburn took a liking to Flood and he quickly rose into leadership roles on important Congressional committees, including subcommittee chairman of the powerful House Appropriations Committee. He used his power and influence to divert federal dollars back to his district. Two of the major pieces of legislation he sponsored were the Area Redevelopment Act of 1961 and the Federal Coal Mine Health and Safety Act of 1969. In addition, the Interstate Highway System was under construction at this time and Congressman Flood saw to it that Interstates 80 and 81 intersected in his district. In fact, it's the only place in the country where the super highways meet.

The year 1972 brought both a challenge and opportunity to Flood when Hurricane Agnes caused massive, believe it or not, *flooding* in his district. The Congressman in the aftermath of the storm is said to have remarked "this will be one Flood against another." He used his clout to get monies through the federal bureaucracy that would normally have been held up. He also pressured authorities for air and boat rescue. He was successful in securing both. He convinced President Nixon to survey the damage which resulted in the President's involvement in the federal response. In the flood's aftermath, his popularity soared.

This was the highpoint of the Congressman's career. As he grew older, health problems slowed him down and he relied more heavily on his staff. In 1979, Flood was indicted on federal bribery and conspiracy charges. A member of the Congressman's staff was the chief prosecution witness. Some have put forward the proposition that the aide turned on Flood to save his own skin, though there is no concrete proof. However, as a result of the allegations, Flood resigned from Congress on January 31, 1980. The case was resolved with Flood pleading guilty to one count of conspiracy for which he was sentenced to one year of probation. Congressman Flood died on May 28th 1994. He was 91 years old. He is buried in Saint Mary's Cemetery in Wilkes-Barre. His grave is easily located as it sits on the left side of the road if you use the main entrance to Saint Mary's.

If You Go:

Also buried in Saint Mary's cemetery is Pete Grey who played major league baseball in 1945, despite having only one arm. Grey had lost his arm in an accident during his youth, but he continued to play baseball learning to throw and hit using his left arm. In the majors, Grey played in 77 games and had 51 hits in 234 at bats. To locate his grave, the authors suggest that you visit the cemetery office to obtain directions. In addition, if you are at

Saint Mary's there is another cemetery in the area in the area you may wish to visit. Mary Jo Kopechne is buried in Saint Vincent's Catholic Cemetery located in Larksville (See Chapter 13). You should also check out the "If You Go" section of chapter 6, "Half the Horseman".

Here lies Congressman Dapper Dan Flood, who took on the flooding caused by Hurricane Agnes as if it had been personally aimed at him.

8.
"The First American"

Benjamin Franklin
County: Philadelphia
Town: Philadelphia
Cemetery: Christ Church Burial Ground
Address: Corner of 5th and Arch Streets

It is not exaggerating to say that to this day, no Pennsylvanian is as well known or as well respected as Ben Franklin. The man excelled at so many things. He was an author, a political theorist, a scientist, an inventor, a diplomat and politician (though he might disagree), and a revolutionary. He truly earned the title "The First American."

Ben Franklin was born in Boston, Massachusetts on January 17, 1706. His father, Josiah Franklin, was born in England where he married his first wife in 1677. The couple arrived in America in 1683. By that time, they had three children, and after arriving in America, they had four more. Josiah made a living as a soap and candle-maker. After his first wife died, he remarried and had ten more children. Franklin was Josiah's 15th child and his last son.

Franklin's parents wanted a career in the church for him. He was sent to school with the clergy but after two years, his parents could no longer make the payments to allow him to continue. Franklin never graduated, but through his own reading, he continued what would be called a self-education. At the age of twelve he went to work for his brother James, a printer, who taught him the trade. James founded "The New England Courant," the first independent newspaper in the colonies. Franklin began to write letters to the paper under the name of Mrs. Silence Dogwood. The views expressed became the subject of conversation around Boston. When James discovered that Franklin was the popular author, he punished him. In addition to verbal abuse, his brother was known to beat Franklin. Having had enough, Franklin fled his apprenticeship at age seventeen, and according to the laws of the time, became a fugitive.

Franklin arrived in Philadelphia in 1723, seeking a fresh start. With his experience, he was able to find work in printing shops. Pennsylvania's Royal Governor William Keith convinced Franklin to return to England to find the equipment needed to start a new newspaper in Philadelphia. When the Governor failed to provide the backing for the enterprise, Franklin found

Benjamin Franklin

work in a printer's shop in London. He returned to Philadelphia in 1726, and went to work for a merchant as a clerk, shopkeeper, and a bookkeeper.

Franklin organized a group of men known as the "Junto" in 1727. The goal of the group was to engage in activities that would improve the members as individuals and at the same time benefit the community. The group created a library. Franklin came up with the idea to form a subscription library, in order to increase the number of books available. This was done by combining the funds of the members to buy additional books that would be available for all to read. Franklin hired the first librarian in 1732.

In 1728, Franklin's employer passed away and Franklin returned to the printing business. The next year, he became the publisher of a newspaper called "The Pennsylvania Gazette." The newspaper provided Franklin with a mechanism to make known his views on the important issues of the time. His observations were well received and his stature continued to grow.

In 1730, Franklin entered into what would be called a common law marriage with Deborah Reed. He could not marry Reed because she already had a husband, though he had abandoned her. One of the reasons that may have led Franklin to make this decision was the fact that he had recently acknowledged that he was the father of an illegitimate son named William, and he wanted to provide his son a family life. William's mother remains unknown. Ben and Deborah had two other children. The first was a son named Francis, who was born in 1732, and died in 1736. The second child, a daughter named Sarah, was born in 1743.

During this time period, Franklin also began a career as an author. In 1733, he began to publish "Poor Richard's Almanac." Franklin seldom published under his own name and in this instance the author was identified as Richard Saunders. Some of his witty adages such as "Fish and visitors stink in three days" are still quoted today. Though published under the name Saunders, it was common knowledge that Franklin was the author. His reputation continued to grow. The almanac itself was a tremendous success, selling about 10,000 copies per year. In today's world, that would translate to about three million copies.

Franklin founded the American Philosophical Society in 1743. The purpose of this organization was to provide a forum where scientific men, like himself, could discuss their projects and discoveries. It was around this time that Franklin began studying electricity. That study would remain a part of his life until the day he died. The story of the kite, the string, and the key is probably a false one. The television show "MythBusters" simulated the supposed experiment and concluded that if Franklin had proceeded as described, he would have been killed.

In addition to his scientific studies, Franklin was also an inventor. Among his more noted inventions are the Franklin stove, the lightning rod, and bifocal lenses. Franklin, viewed his inventions as yet another way that life could be improved for humankind.

In 1747, Franklin decided to get out of the printing business. He formed a partnership whereby David Hall would run the business and the two would share the profits. This provided Franklin with a steady income and also gave him the time to pursue his studies and other interests. His writings, inventions, and discoveries had by now made him well known throughout the colonies and in Europe.

As he grew older, Franklin became more and more interested in public affairs. He was drawn into Philadelphia politics and was soon elected to the post of councilman. In 1749 he became a Justice of the Peace and two years later, he was elected to the Pennsylvania Assembly. In 1753, he was appointed to the post of joint deputy postmaster general of North America. In this role, he worked to reform the postal system. Among his accomplishments was the adoption of the practice to deliver mail on a weekly basis.

During this time, Franklin founded the first hospital in the colonies. Honors continued to come his way. In 1753, both Harvard and Yale awarded him honorary degrees. In 1757, the Pennsylvania Assembly selected Franklin to go to England to oppose the political favoritism that was being shown to the Penn family who were descended from Pennsylvania's founder William Penn. The family was exempt from paying any land taxes and retained the right to veto legislation passed by the Pennsylvania Assembly. Franklin worked on this mission for five years but it ended in failure as the Royal government refused to turn their backs on the Penn family.

During his stay in England, more honors came his way. In 1759, the University of Saint Andrews awarded him an honorary degree. Three years later, Oxford followed suit by awarding Franklin an honorary doctorate for his scientific achievements. It was as a result of this award that he became known as Doctor Franklin. To top it off, he also secured an appointment for his illegitimate son William. The younger Franklin was named Colonial Governor of New Jersey.

When Franklin returned to America, the feud between the Penn's and the Assembly was ongoing. Franklin became leader of the anti-Penn party known as the anti-propriety party. In 1764 he was elected Speaker of the Pennsylvania House. As speaker, Franklin attempted to change Pennsylvania from a propriety to a royal government. The move was not popular with the voting populous who feared that such a change would infringe on their freedoms. As a result, Franklin was defeated in the elections held in October of 1764. After his defeat, the anti-propriety party sent him back to England to try yet again to fight the influence of the Penn family.

While in London, Franklin spoke out in opposition to the Stamp Act of 1765, but the measure passed over his objections. This did not deter him, and he continued to fight the act. His efforts contributed to its eventual repeal. As a result, he became the leading representative for American interests in England.

During his time in Europe, Franklin decided to tour Ireland. This visit would have a profound effect on him. When he witnessed the poverty in Ireland, he became convinced that it was a result of regulations and laws similar to those through which England was governing America. He came to the conclusion that America would suffer a fate similar to Ireland's if England's colonial exploitation continued.

Franklin's common law wife never accompanied him overseas because of her fear of the ocean. While he was on this trip, she implored him to return to America. She claimed she was ill and blamed her condition on his absence. Franklin stayed in England and Deborah Reed died as a result of a stroke in 1774.

Franklin returned to America in May of 1775. By this time the American Revolution had already begun with the battles of Lexington and Concord. Pennsylvania selected him as one of their delegates to the Second Continental Congress. While serving in Congress, he was appointed to the committee chosen to draft the Declaration of Independence. Thomas Jefferson did the bulk of the work on the Declaration, though Franklin did make several minor changes to the draft Jefferson provided to the other members of the committee. As the Declaration was signed, the President of Congress, John Hancock, remarked "We must all hang together." Franklin replied, "Yes, we must, indeed, all hang together, or most assuredly we shall all hang separately."

In July of 1775, the Continental Congress appointed Franklin to the post of United States Postmaster General. He was the country's first postmaster. The appointment made sense based on Franklin's previous postal experience. The postal system that was established then evolved into the United States Postal Service that is still operational today.

In 1776, Franklin was sent to France to represent American interests. He was already well known in that country due to his writings, inventions, and scientific discoveries. His appointment bore fruit. Franklin succeeded in securing a military alliance between the United States and France in 1778. This alliance was of critical importance to the Americans in their struggle against England. There are those who doubt that the American Revolution would have succeeded without the help of France. Franklin also played a key role in negotiating the Treaty of Paris in 1783. This treaty ended the American Revolution and established the United States as an independent country.

Franklin returned to the United States in 1785. His stature as a champion of American independence was exceeded by only one man, that man being George Washington. That same year, he was elected President of Pennsylvania, a post that would be similar to governor today. Franklin served in this position for just over three years.

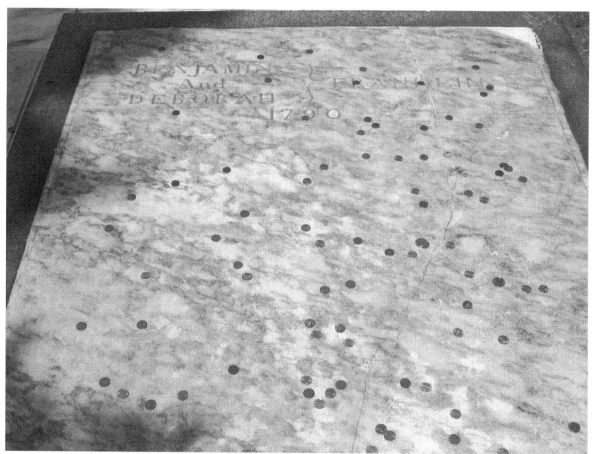

The authors consider this man to be Mister Pennsylvania and Mister America.

In 1787 he was selected to serve as a Pennsylvania delegate at the Constitutional Convention in Philadelphia. For four months, the delegates met and argued over whether the country should establish a strong federal government. On the day the voting on the proposed constitution was to take place, many of the delegates believed it would be voted down. Prior to the voting, Franklin advised the Convention that he had a few comments to make. At the time he was too frail to deliver the speech himself so he had fellow Pennsylvania delegate James Wilson read it for him. In the speech

Franklin spoke of his own misgivings about the Constitution. However in the end he said, "Thus I consent, sir, to this Constitution. The opinions I have of its errors, I sacrifice to the public good." He went on to say, "On the whole, sir, I cannot help expressing a wish that every member of the convention who may still have objections to it would, with me, on this occasion doubt a little of his own infallibility and make manifest our unanimity." When the vote was taken it was close to unanimous. Only three of the forty one delegates refused to sign the document and it was eventually ratified by all thirteen states.

Franklin died in his Philadelphia home on April 17, 1790. He was 84 years old. He is the only founding father who signed all four of the documents central to the establishment of the United States. These are the Declaration of Independence, the Treaty of Paris, the Treaty of Alliance with France, and the United States Constitution. His funeral was attended by an estimated 20,000 people. He was laid to rest in the Christ Church Burial Ground in Philadelphia.

If You Go:

The Christ Church Cemetery charges a modest entry fee. This fee is used to cover the cemeteries maintenance costs. There are a number of other important Americans buried here and maps are available at the cemetery (again for a modest charge) that direct you to their gravesites. If you do make the trip, you are in the midst of Philadelphia's historic district. Both Independence Hall and the Constitution Center are within easy walking distance. In addition, there are many street vendors and numerous restaurants in the area if you desire refreshments. Finally, the Betsy Ross House, which includes her burial site is only about three blocks away.

9.
"An American Success Story Few Have Heard"

John White Geary
County: Dauphin
Town: Harrisburg
Cemetery: Harrisburg
Address: 521 North 13th Street

John Geary has a county in Kansas named for him. Kansas also has a Geary State Park. There is a Geary Boulevard in San Francisco, California named in his honor. There is a Geary street in both New Cumberland (where he owned a home) and Harrisburg, Pennsylvania. Not to be left out, there is a Geary Street in South Philadelphia as well. There is a monument honoring Geary in Mount Pleasant, Pennsylvania. There is a dorm building at the Pennsylvania State University named Geary Hall. Finally, on August 11, 2007, a statue was unveiled on Culp's Hill, which is part of the Gettysburg Battlefield. It was erected to honor Geary. Clearly, the subject of this chapter was a man who got around.

Geary was born on December 30, 1819 in what is today the greater Pittsburgh metropolitan area. His father, Richard Geary, was considered a well educated man. Richard took on the task of educating his two sons. After being prepared by his father, Geary became a student of law and engineering at Jefferson College in Canonsburg, Pennsylvania. Prior to his graduation, his father passed away and he was forced to leave school. He found work in Kentucky as a surveyor. While in Kentucky, he also tried his hand at land speculation. He was successful enough to earn the money he needed to return to college, and he graduated in 1841. Upon graduation, he worked at a number of professions including the mercantile trade and civil engineering. He also studied law and was admitted to the state bar.

In 1843, Geary married Margaret Ann Logan. In 1846, his first son Edward was born. During this time, Geary was employed by the Alleghany Portage Rail Road as an engineer. He was instrumental in creating the rail line that traversed the Alleghany mountains. His ideas would later be used in the construction of the famed horseshoe curve.

Geary was already a high ranking officer in the Pennsylvania militia when the Mexican War began in 1846. He formed a company he called the "American Highlanders", all volunteers and all from Cambria County. This unit was joined with a company from Pittsburgh and Geary was elected second in command.

John White Geary (by Mathew Brady)

The combined unit sailed for Mexico, but encountered delays due to both weather and disease. As they approached the Gulf of Mexico, a few cases of smallpox appeared and the ship was sent to be quarantined. Finally, all signs of the disease disappeared and on April 12, 1847, Geary and the rest of the company arrived in Vera Cruz. By this time that city had already been taken by the Americans, so he had to wait for the Battle at Chapultepec to lead his men into an actual engagement with the enemy. He performed heroically, and was wounded multiple times during the battle. Considering that he stood at six foot six inches tall and weighed 260 pounds, he must have made for an inviting target. At the war's conclusion, Geary had earned the rank of colonel and returned to the United States a hero of the Mexican War.

After the war, President Polk appointed Geary postmaster of San Francisco. Geary embarked for the west coast with his three year old son, his pregnant wife, and thousands of pieces of mail. He and his family arrived in 1849 at the height of the gold rush. He quickly dove into his duties establishing post offices, mail routes, and appointing postmasters. His management skill earned him the admiration of the local citizens. Despite his success in this office, President Taylor, who succeeded Polk, replaced Geary as postmaster.

It appears that the people of San Francisco did not agree with the new president. In 1850, Geary was easily elected the first mayor of the city. He remains the youngest mayor in San Francisco's history. By this time, due to his wife's failing health, Geary had sent her and his two sons back to Pennsylvania. He remained in California where he governed capably. He worked hard to get the city's finances in order and was successful. At the same time, he added to his own fortune by selling city lots he acquired at little cost to him. In 1852, he returned to Pennsylvania to be with his family and care for his wife. It was to no avail as she passed away in 1853. Geary would remarry in 1858.

At this point in his life, Geary was determined to devout himself to farming and his various business pursuits. This was not to be. His reputation as a war hero and capable administrator led to President Pierce offering him the governorship of the Kansas territory in 1856. At the time "Bleeding Kansas", as it was called, was a battleground between pro and anti slavery forces. Geary was not eager to accept the position but acquiesced when Pierce appealed to his patriotic spirit.

In this instance Geary's initial reluctance may have been correct. His predecessor as governor remarked, "that to govern Kansas in 1855 and 1856, you might as well have attempted to govern the devil in hell." Bleak were the conditions Geary inherited when he arrived in Kansas on September 9, 1856. The Kansas territory was practically a war zone over the issue of slavery. The new governor pledged to be impartial and fair in dealing with the opposition factions in the territory. This policy resulted in the further alienation of both sides.

Geary's problems in Kansas were complicated by the fact that many of President Pierce's appointees in the territory were solidly pro slavery. These officials resisted Geary's efforts to enforce the law, and bring peace to Kansas. Geary wrote to the president requesting the removal of multiple judges, and the replacement of the Federal Marshall, the Secretary of State, and the Attorney General. With a presidential campaign in progress, Pierce determined that the best course was to let his successor handle the problem. James Buchanan of Pennsylvania, who had no record on the issues in Kansas, won the election. Geary clearly lacked confidence in the new president, and he tendered his resignation on March 4, 1857. It was the very day Buchanan was inaugurated. Later in recalling his Kansas experience, Geary wrote, "I have learned more about the depravity of my fellow man than I ever knew before."

After his time in Kansas Geary returned to Pennsylvania where he met Mary Church Henderson of Carlisle. Soon, the two were married. In a short time, they welcomed their first child, a girl who they named Mary.

Although Geary was a staunch Democrat, he was also firmly anti-slavery. As soon as Geary received word that rebel forces had fired on Fort Sumter, he began recruiting troops. He set up recruiting stations in Philadelphia and elsewhere. Based on his reputation, he had little trouble securing volunteers. Sixty-six companies from all over the Commonwealth requested to be put under his command. In the end, Geary formed a 15 company regiment. He and his men saw their first action in October 1861, near Harpers Ferry. In 1862, he led his men across the Potomac and captured the rebel town of Leesburg, Virginia. As a result, Geary was promoted to Brigadier General.

Later that year, Geary faced rebel forces under the command of Stonewall Jackson during the Battle of Cedar Mountain. Geary was wounded in both the arm and the leg during the fighting. The wound to the arm was so severe that amputation was considered. While amputation was avoided, Geary was forced to return home to rest and recover.

When Geary returned to the army, he was put in command of the Second Division of the twelfth Corps under General Slocum. Geary would remain in charge of this division until the war's end. Geary's men saw plenty of action performing heroically at both Chancellorsville and Gettysburg. It was at Gettysburg atop Culp's Hill that Geary and his men repulsed repeated confederate assaults and succeeded in holding the union's right flank. The action on Culp's hill cemented Geary's reputation as a civil war hero. However, the man was not one to rest on his laurels.

Geary's monument stands where he fought, atop Culp's Hill on the Gettysburg battlefield.

In September of 1863, Geary's division was sent to Tennessee to join the forces of Generals Grant and Sherman. On October 27, 1863, Geary's forces were attacked by a superior force of confederates. In an intense battle known as the Battle of Wauhatchie, the union forces turned back repeated confederate assaults. During the fighting, Geary's son Eddie was mortally wounded. He died in his father's arms, but Geary and his men held their ground.

Geary's division went on to fight in the Battle of Lookout Mountain, the Atlanta campaign, and Sherman's march to the sea. He led the union forces into Savannah where he was appointed military governor of the city. He ended his army career by serving on the military tribunal that tried Major Henry Wirtz, who had served as commandant of the Andersonville prisoner of war camp. Wirtz was found guilty of war crimes and was hanged in December of 1865.

Geary now returned to Pennsylvania. Though he had always been a democrat, powerful elements of the republican party began looking at him as a potential candidate for governor. Supported by the former Secretary of War, Simon Cameron, Geary was selected to head the republican ticket in Pennsylvania. He won the election by 17,000 votes and was inaugurated governor in Harrisburg on January 15, 1867.

Geary served two successful terms as governor. He championed education and was a big supporter of Penn State University. He also worked against the influence of the railroads, and for improvements in mine safety. His policies resulted in a reduced public debt and an increase in revenues. He left the state in a far better condition than he had found it when he left the governor's office in 1873.

No sooner than Geary left office, rumors began to circulate that he was considering a run for president. That was not to be. Less than three weeks after leaving the office of govenor, on February 8, 1873, Geary suffered a massive heart attack and died while preparing breakfast at his home. He was 54 years old.

Geary was given a state funeral that included speeches from the political leaders of the Commonwealth. The funeral was followed by a large procession to the Harrisburg cemetery where he was laid to rest. His grave is marked by a monument that is topped by a statue of the great man. It is the only statue in the cemetery and was erected by the Commonwealth of Pennsylvania.

If You Go:

See the "If You Go" section in Chapter 5 on Simon Cameron.

Geary's grave in the Harrisburg Cemetery is the only one topped by a statue. The monument was erected by the Commonwealth of Pennsylvania.

10.
"What Does it All Mean?"

Frank Gorshin
County: Allegheny
Town: Pittsburgh
Cemetery: Calvary
Address: 718 Hazelwood Avenue

Riddle me this. A famous actor, both stage and screen, a fantastic impressionist, a well known nightclub performer, and a featured guest star on numerous variety television shows who is best known for his role in the campy television series "Batman." If you answered Frank Gorshin, you solved the riddle. To this day he is most closely associated with his role as the Riddler.

Frank Gorshin was born in Pittsburgh, Pennsylvania on April 5, 1933. He was born during the Great Depression and both his parents worked. His mother was a seamstress and his father was employed by the railroad. When he was 15, Frank found employment himself, working as an usher at the Sheridan Square Movie Theatre in Pittsburgh. While watching the movies, he began to impersonate his favorite stars. Soon he was doing Jimmy Cagney, Cary Grant, Burt Lancaster, and Edward G. Robinson among others. At the age of 17 he won a local talent contest. First prize was a one week engagement at a New York nightclub, the Carousel. His parents said he should do the show, and he did, even though his 15 year old brother had been hit by a car and killed just two days earlier. While his entertainment career was underway, he also attended school at the Carnegie-Mellon Tech School of Drama where he acted in plays while at the same time performing in Pittsburgh nightclubs.

In 1953, Gorshin was drafted into the United States Army. He served two years in the Armed Forces. His primary job in the army was to entertain the troops. He did, however, meet a man by the name of Maurice Bergman while he was there. At the completion of Frank's tour, Bergman, introduced him to Paul Kohner, a Hollywood agent.

It was at this point that Gorshin's career took off. He landed a film role in "The Proud and the Profane." He also began appearing in television dramas. He was at home in Pittsburgh in 1957, when his agent called and said he had a screen test set up for him for the movie "Run Silent Run Deep." He decided to drive back to Hollywood, but after 39 straight hours, he fell asleep at the wheel and crashed. He suffered a fractured skull in the accident and was in a coma for four days. One Los Angeles newspaper mistakenly reported that he had died in the crash. He lost the part to Don Rickles.

Actor Frank Gorshin

After he recovered from the accident, Gorshin appeared in a string of B-movies from 1956 through 1960. These movies included "Dragstrip Girl," "Invasion of the Saucer Men," and "Hot Rod Girl." He also married Christina Randazzo in 1957, and though they eventually separated, they were never divorced. In 1960, he landed a role in a mainstream movie titled "Bells Are Ringing" which starred Dean Martin and Judy Holiday. Gorshin would later make numerous appearances on Martin's TV variety show. In 1961, he appeared in the movie "The Great Imposter" that starred Tony Curtis.

In early 1964, Gorshin made his first appearance (there would be twelve in all) on The Ed Sullivan Show. Among the other acts making their first appearance on the show that night was a musical group called The Beatles and a young fellow by the name of Davy Jones who later became part of the made for TV musical group The Monkees.

In 1966, Gorshin was offered the role of the Riddler on the TV show Batman. He told the story himself: "When I was first approached to play the Riddler, I thought it was a joke. Then I discovered the show had a good script and I agreed to do the role…" We think it's good to remember at this point that Gorshin had agreed to do 'Invasion of the Saucer Men'. He continued with, "Now I am in love with the character. I developed the Riddler's fiendish laugh at Hollywood parties. I listened to myself laugh and discovered that the funniest jokes brought out the high-pitched giggle I use on the show. With further study, I came to realize that it wasn't so much how I laughed as what I laughed at that created the sense of menace." Whatever it was, it worked. Gorshin was nominated for an Emmy award for Outstanding Performance by an Actor in a Supporting Role in a Comedy. Gorshin was the only person who appeared in the series to receive a nomination. Later, he recalled that he "could feel the impact overnight." He gained recognition nationwide and soon became a headliner in Vegas. In 1969, he received another Emmy nomination this time for his performance as Commissioner Bele in a Star Trek episode called "Let That Be Your Last Battlefield."

Gorshin also appeared on Broadway. In 1970, he starred in the play "Jimmy" based on New York's flamboyant Mayor Jimmy Walker. He received fantastic reviews. In 1971, he appeared in "Guys and Dolls." His final appearance on the Broadway stage was in a one man play titled "Say Goodnight Gracie" in 2002. He portrayed the legendary comedian George Burns in the production.

He stayed active in his final years. His last job was a guest appearance on the season finale of CSI: Crime Investigation in an episode titled "Grave Danger." Quenton Tarantino was the director. Some find it ironic that the man so well known for his impressions played himself in this episode. It aired two days after he died and was dedicated to his memory.

Batman's arch enemy "the Riddler" lies beneath this stone. Though in our view his talents exceeded anything he did on that TV show. ("Ghost" of the co-author in reflection!)

Gorshin died on May 17, 2005, at the age of 72. He had taken a flight to Los Angeles and upon landing was rushed to a hospital. He died from lung cancer, emphysema, and pneumonia. He is buried in his family's plot in Calvary Cemetery in Pittsburgh.

If You Go:

We would strongly suggest you visit the cemetery office to obtain directions to the graves you might want to visit at Calvary. It's a very large cemetery and without guidance you could be there for days. For more information on who is buried in Calvary and what you can do in Pittsburgh see chapter 6 on "Half the Horsemen."

Zane Grey as a member of the Penn's baseball team (1895-6)

11.
"Rider of the Purple Sage"

Zane Grey
County: Pike
Cemetery: Lackawaxen and Union Cemetery
Address: Lackawaxen

Zane Grey was an American author. He is best known for his adventure novels and stories that presented an idealized image of the old west. While he authored many westerns, his work also includes books about hunting and fishing, six juvenile books, short stories and baseball stories. His best known novel is "Riders of the Purple Sage."

From 1915 to 1924 a Grey book was in the top 10 on the best sellers list every year except 1916. He was published in hardcover, serialized in magazines and reissued in paperback editions. Hollywood turned 46 of his books into movies beginning in 1912 and continuing to the present day. A television series "Dick Powell's Zane Grey Theater" ran from 1956 to 1960 and produced 145 episodes.

When Grey was born in 1872 in Zanesville, Ohio, his parents named him Pearl Zane Gray. His family decided to change the spelling to Grey after his birth. Later he abandoned the name Pearl and used Zane as a first name.

He studied dentistry at the University of Pennsylvania, which he attended on a baseball scholarship, and he graduated in 1896. After graduation he established a practice in New York City. During this period he also played amateur baseball while concentrating on writing in the evenings. He had offers to play professional baseball but turned them down because his burning ambition was to become a writer.

Grey was very close to his younger brother Romer and they frequently fished in Lackawaxen, Pennsylvania on the Delaware river. It was there, in 1900, he met the woman who would become his wife. Her name was Lina Roth but he preferred to call her Dolly. They married in 1905 and moved to a farmhouse in Lackawaxen, where Grey devoted himself to writing full time.

His first novel titled "Betty Zane" was rejected by every publisher to which it was submitted. He published it himself, but ended up losing money due to the costs. In 1910, Harper's magazine published "The Heritage of the Desert." It became a bestseller and was the prototype of all Zane Grey westerns. Two years later he wrote "Riders of the Purple Sage" which became the most successful western novel ever published.

Despite his success, Grey had problems he had to overcome. He suffered bouts of depression and mood swings throughout his life. One of his coping mechanisms was to engage in his favorite activity, fishing, as it seemed to provide him comfort. When he became financially successful, he indulged in fishing all over the world. This led to regular stories written for "Outdoor Life" magazine that helped popularize big-game fishing.

In 1916, Hollywood bought the rights to "Riders of the Purple Sage". Two years later, the Grey family moved to California to be closer to the film

Who would have ever thought that this Rider of the Purple Sage would wind up buried in Pennsylvania?

industry and to enable Grey to fish the Pacific. The move proved to be a wise one as, over the years, nearly fifty of his novels were made into more than one hundred movies. Famous actors such as Gary Cooper, Randolph Scott, Buster Crabbe, and William Holden got their start in these films.

Grey became one of the world's first millionaire authors. He wrote more than ninety books, including some that were published after his death. His total book sales are said to be over forty million.

Zane Grey died of heart failure on October 23, 1939 at his home in Altadena, California. He was 67 years old. He is buried in a modest grave, in a small cemetery, in Lackawaken, Pennsylvania called the Lackawaxen and Union Cemetery.

If You Go:

Zane Grey's former home in Lackawaxen is now a museum operated by the National Park Service. It contains memorabilia, photographs, and books in the rooms that served as his office and study. The museum is open on a seasonal basis, usually Memorial Day to Labor Day. Unfortunately, it was not open when we made our visit.

12.
"That Ball's Outta Here"

Harry Norbert Kalas
County: Philadelphia
Town: Philadelphia
Cemetery: Laurel Hill Cemetery
Address: 3822 Ridge Avenue

"That ball is outta here" was Harry Kalas' home run call, and it has become one of the legendary baseball calls. Harry Kalas was a Hall of Fame broadcaster best known for his role as lead play-by-play announcer for the Philadelphia Phillies. He also was well known as the voice of NFL films from 1975 until his death.

Kalas was born in Naperville, Illinois on March 26, 1936. He graduated from Naperville High School in 1954. He made the University of Iowa his college choice, graduating in 1959. Soon after he left the university, he was drafted into the United States Army. He was stationed in Hawaii where he served until he was discharged in 1961. It was at this point that Harry began his illustrious broadcasting career, calling minor league baseball games for the Hawaii Islanders.

In 1965, he was hired by the Houston Astros to broadcast their games. He remained there until the Phillies hired him in 1971. Initially, his hiring was not met with the approval of a number of Phillies fans. The man he replaced, Bill Campbell, was extremely popular among the team's fan base. Kalas won the fans over quickly. His easy going style that would all of a sudden register great excitement when a Phillie made a great play in the field or delivered a key hit turned Campbell into a fond memory.

Kalas was the Master of Ceremonies at the opening of Veteran's Stadium. He also called the last game at the "Vet" and the first game at Citizens Bank Park. He was eventually paired up with Hall of Fame player Richie Ashburn (who will appear in a subsequent volume) and the duo became best friends as well as sports icons in Philadelphia. He and Ashburn broadcast together for 27 seasons until Ashburn's death in 1997.

During his Phillies career Kalas broadcast six no-hitters, six National League Championship Series, and three World Series. He missed broadcasting the 1980 World Series because of a Major League Baseball rule that prohibited local broadcasters from calling the series due to conflict with the networks. As a result of a public outcry the rule was changed. By now,

Tomb of Harry Kalas in Lauel Hill Cemetery

Kalas had clearly made a national name for himself.

Kalas was nicknamed "Harry the K" by Phillies fans and loved the Frank Sinatra song "High Hopes" which he sang on many occasions. The year before his passing, Harry had the opportunity to broadcast the ultimate highlight: calling the game as his beloved Phillies won the World Series and became "the 2008 World Champions of Baseball" He then joined the on-field celebration, grabbing a microphone and belting out "High Hopes".

To a whole generation of football fans, Kalas was known as the voice of "Inside The NFL". He did the voiceover from 1977 through 2008. In addition to his work with the Phillies and NFL films, Kalas called various sports over the years for the Mutual Broadcasting System, CBS Radio, and Westwood One. This included NFL games, Major league Baseball, college basketball, and Notre Dame football. For many years, he narrated the "Alcoa

Gravesite of the legendary Phillie and NFL announcer. Note grave goods behind box seats on right side of photo.

Fantastic Finishes" in game highlight spots for use during NFL telecasts.

On April 8, 2009, the Philadelphia Phillies honored Kalas by having him throw out the first pitch before a game with the Atlanta Braves. The Phillies received their championship rings as part of the ceremony. It turned out to be the last home game Harry Kalas ever announced. Kalas collapsed in the press box as he was preparing to broadcast a game between the Phillies and Washington Nationals at National's Park. He died on April 13, 2009 at George Washington University Hospital at the age of 73. For the rest of the season, the Phillies wore a patch on their uniforms that bore the initials "HK".

Kalas received the Ford Frick Award from the National Baseball Hall of Fame in 2002. In June 2009, he was inducted into the National Radio

Hall of Fame and Museum. He was named Pennsylvania Broadcaster of the Year 18 times.

He is buried in historic Laurel Hill Cemetery overlooking the Schuylkill River. His tombstone is shaped like a giant microphone with the letters "HK" in the middle and a likeness of Kalas' autograph at the microphone's base which sits on top of a raised base shaped like home plate and is flanked on each side by a pair of seats from Veterans Stadium. In 2010, the grave was resurfaced with sod that originally came from Citizens Bank Park. When we visited his grave, visitors had left baseballs there, some autographed, and there were numerous coins as well.

If You Go:

There are several interesting and famous graves in Laurel Hill Cemetery (see Chapter 19 on George Meade).

Henry Deringer, who is interred here, was developer of one of the most famous American guns the derringer, designed to be compact and easily concealed. John Wilkes Booth used a derringer to assassinate Abraham Lincoln.

Boies Penrose is also buried nearby. He was a US Senator from 1897-1921. There is a prominent large statue of Penrose on the grounds of the Pennsylvania State Capitol, although it is hard to understand why. The statute shows Penrose with his hand in one pocket. Many from Pennsylvania claim it's not lifelike because Boies never had his hand in his own pocket.

The cemetery itself is located very near the Philadelphia Zoo and the city's art museum. Both deserve a visit. While it is hard to recommend where to stop and dine in Philly (there are so many great places), we had a great lunch at a spot close to the cemetery called the Trolley Car Café on S. Ferry Road. It featured delicious gourmet salads, sandwiches, and soups and offered a patio setting if you wished to move outside.

Close-up of grave goods left by visitors to Harry the K's grave.

13.
"What If?"

Mary Jo Kopechne
County: Luzerne
Town: Larksville
Cemetery: Saint Vincents Cemetery
Address: Washington Avenue

Mary Jo Kopechne, far left during 1967 staff meeting with RFK.

The subject of this chapter is different than anyone else appearing in this volume. Mary Jo Kopechne is famous as a result of the way she died. Virtually everyone else in the book gained their fame through the things they accomplished while living. It is a fact that nobody can say how different America, and for that matter, world history might have been had Kopechne lived.

Mary Jo Kopechne was born in Wilkes-Barre, Pennsylvania on July 26, 1940. While she was still an infant, her family relocated to New Jersey. In terms of her education through High School, she was a product of the parochial school system. When it came time to choose a college Mary Jo decided on the Caldwell College for Women which is also located in New Jersey. She graduated in 1962 with a degree in business administration.

After graduation, Kopechne's first job was teaching at the Mission of Saint Jude in Montgomery, Alabama. In 1963, she moved to Washington, D. C., to work for Florida Senator George Smathers. Smathers was a close friend of John F. Kennedy, and he may have assisted Mary Jo in moving to Robert Kennedy's staff when he was elected Senator by the people of New York in 1964.

Kopechne was a loyal Robert Kennedy employee right up until the time of his death. When Kennedy decided to run for president in 1968 she went to work on his campaign. She worked with a group of women that became known as the "Boiler Room Girls", a nickname the six women earned because the office they worked in was hot and had no windows. Among their duties was tracking democratic delegates and how they intended to vote. One of the states that fell under Kopechne's responsibility was Pennsylvania.

On June 5, 1968, Robert Kennedy was assassinated. Kopechne was devastated and, at first, claimed she couldn't return to Washington. However, in December 1968, she was hired by Matt Reese Associates, a political consulting firm based in Washington. Through her work for the firm she soon found that she was on her way to a successful career.

By this time, Robert Kennedy's younger brother and senator from Massachusetts, Edward Moore Kennedy was already being mentioned as a potential candidate for president in either 1972 or 1976. Edward was commonly known as Ted or Teddy Kennedy and he had already turned down the chance to be a vice-presidential candidate in 1968. Many political pundits held the opinion that it was just a matter of time until the youngest of the Kennedy brothers would be elected president.

On July 18, 1969, Ted Kennedy hosted a party on Chappaquiddick Island, just off the Massachusetts coast to honor the Boiler Room Girls. It is impossible to say with any certainty what happened that night and in the early morning hours of the next day. According to Kennedy, at about 11:15

p.m. he indicated he was going to leave the party. He said that Kopechne asked him if he could drop her off at her hotel. Kennedy then obtained the car keys from his chauffer. When asked why he didn't have the chauffer drive them both he said that the chauffeur was finishing his meal and he didn't see a reason to disturb him. Kennedy and Kopechne left the party. Mary Jo did not inform her friends she was leaving and she failed to take either her purse or her hotel key with her. Kennedy said he was driving the car, a 1967 Oldsmobile, when he took a wrong turn onto Dike Road. He said he was driving at about twenty miles an hour when he came to a wooden bridge known as Dike Bridge that had no guardrails. Immediately before reaching the bridge Kennedy hit his brakes and then drove off the side of the structure. His car ended up upside down underwater in Poucha Pond. Kennedy said he escaped the vehicle, though he could not remember how. He called out for Kopechne and getting no response he claimed he repeatedly dove into the water but that his attempts to reach the vehicle were unsuccessful. He then said that he rested for a time before returning on foot to the Lawrence Cottage, where the party was being held.

According to his testimony, Kennedy denied seeing any houses with their lights on as he walked back to the party. According to others, he would have passed four houses on his way back to the party. The first of these residences was known as "Dike's House". It was 150 yards from the bridge. Sylvia Malm, who was living there at the time stated that she had left lights on in the house when she retired for the evening and that she had a working telephone. There was also a working telephone in the Lawrence Cottage.

The men at the party included Kennedy cousin, Joseph Gargan, and a friend of Gargan's named Paul Markham. According to Kennedy, he, Gargan, and Markham returned to the scene of the accident. Again attempts by all three men to reach the vehicle were unsuccessful. Gargan and Markham then drove Kennedy to the ferry landing though the last ferry had left for the evening. Both told Kennedy he needed to report the accident. Reportedly Kennedy responded, "You two take care of the girls, and I will take care of the accident." He then dove into the water, swam across the 500-foot channel, and returned to his hotel room. Gargan and Markham later took the position that they did not report the accident because they assumed Kennedy was going to do it.

At 8 a.m. the following day Gargan and Markham arrived at Kennedy's hotel room. According to his testimony, Kennedy said the two asked him why he had not reported the accident. He claimed that as he swam the channel he began to believe that somehow it would be found out that Mary Jo had survived. The three men then took the ferry back to Chappaquiddick where Kennedy made calls to friends, from a pay phone, requesting advice. The accident remained unreported.

That morning, fishermen spotted the automobile submerged in the water. They went to a nearby cottage and the residents notified the authorities. It was about 8:20 a.m. The Edgartown Police Chief James Arena, responded arriving in about 15 minutes. When his attempts to examine the interior of the vehicle were unsuccessful, he called a diver and a truck with towing capability. The diver, a man named Jim Farrar, arrived dressed in his scuba gear and recovered Mary Jo's body in about 10 minutes. He also checked the license plate and found that it was registered to Kennedy.

Shortly, the news reached Kennedy that the car and Mary Jo's body had been discovered. At this point, he took the ferry back to Edgartown and went to the police station to report the accident. When he arrived at the station, he made a few more phone calls before submitting a statement to the police. The statement, much of which has been covered above, created more questions than it answered.

Seven days after the incident, Ted Kennedy pleaded guilty to leaving the scene of an accident after causing injury. Judge James Boyle sentenced Kennedy to two months in jail but he promptly suspended the sentence, citing Kennedy's unblemished record. In his remarks, the judge noted that Kennedy "would continue to be punished beyond anything this court could impose." No one knows whether the judge was referring to the guilt Kennedy would be required to carry, or to the damage done to his political career.

There are many unanswered questions from the incident. John Farrar, the diver who recovered Mary Jo's body, claimed that her death was caused by suffocation and not by drowning. He said Kopechne had positioned her body to take advantage of an air pocket in the vehicle. It was his belief that if he had been called to the scene in a timely manner Mary Jo would have survived.

There is yet another interesting possibility as to what took place that night. A deputy sheriff by the name of Christopher "Huck" Look was working as a special officer that night due to the various celebrations related to the Edgartown Regatta. He was driving home at about 12:40 a.m. when he saw a parked car containing a man and a woman stopped on a private road. Thinking the couple might be lost he went to offer assistance. He stopped his vehicle and at a distance of twenty to thirty feet began walking toward the car. The car started up and moved by him quickly. Look later recalled that the license plate contained an "L" and two "7"s a description that matched Kennedy's vehicle.

There are those that have put forth the theory that after eluding the deputy sheriff, Kennedy left the car and walked back to the party. Meanwhile, Kopechne, being unfamiliar with the area, drove off the bridge instead of returning to the party. The proponents of this theory argue that it accounts for Kennedy's lack of concern until the vehicle was discovered.

Whatever actually happened, it altered Kennedy's political life forever. While the people of the Bay State never turned on him, many of those outside Massachusetts never really trusted him again. He did not run for the presidency in 1972 or 1976. When he did run in 1980 against an incumbent president who was a member of his own party, he failed. In running against Kennedy, President Jimmy Carter often repeated that "he

Here lies a woman whose death may have changed American and World history.

had never panicked in a crisis." For the remainder of his life Ted Kennedy remained the senior senator from Massachusetts. By all accounts he served his state well and was well respected by his fellow senators.

Mary Jo Kopechne died when she was just shy of her 29th birthday. She is buried in Saint Vincent's Cemetery in Larksville, Pennsylvania. As you enter the cemetery, you will notice a main section that makes its way up a modest hill. Mary Jo is about a quarter of the way up right in the middle of the main section.

If You Go:

You are close to the final resting places of two people covered in this volume. See Chapter 7 on Congressman Dan Flood and Chapter 6 titled "Half the Horsemen" on Jim Crowley.

14.
"Pittsburgh's Renaissance Man"

David L. Lawrence
County: Allegheny
Town: Pittsburgh
Cemetery: Calvary
Address: 718 Hazelwood Avenue

American cities and states have had their share of political bosses. The state of New Jersey produced Frank Hague. In Boston, James Michael Curley threw his political weight around. Huey Long from Louisiana had movies made about him. Tom Pendergast backed Harry Truman out of Missouri and into the White House. Richard Daley was the giant of Chicago politics for years. Pennsylvania produced David Lawrence whose biography is ironically titled "Don't Call Me Boss."

David Lawrence was born in Pittsburgh, Pennsylvania on June 18, 1889. His parents were working class Irish Catholics. His father had an interest in politics particularly in supporting his neighborhood and fellow workers. His mother demanded high morals and self-discipline and both parents were important in shaping his character. The family could not afford to send Lawrence to college, so in 1903, he took a job as a clerk for a Pittsburgh attorney named William Brennan. Brennan was active in the labor movement and chairman of the Pittsburgh Democratic party, and he took Lawrence under his wing. Through Brennan, Lawrence grew to love Pennsylvania Democratic politics. He attended his first Democratic National Convention in 1912. He would not miss another until the day he died. In 1916, he entered into an insurance agency partnership with State Senator Frank Harris. He eventually bought Mr. Harris out and the company provided him with a safety net as he pursued a career in politics. In 1918, during World War I, Lawrence enlisted in the army and served as an officer in the adjutant general's office in Washington, D.C.

In 1919, he returned home from the military and was elected chairman of the Allegheny County Democratic Party. For the next twelve years he devoted himself to building a democratic power base. When he was finished, he had created a machine that would dominate local and state elections.

Lawrence married Alyce Golden on June 8, 1921. They eventually had five children, three sons and two daughters. Unfortunately two of the sons

"Pennsylvania's Political Poker Room" cartoon from 1938. Governor Lawrence is seated to the right.

were killed in an automobile accident. Their deaths would result in Lawrence making traffic safety a central part of his agenda when he became governor.

In 1931, Lawrence ran for county commissioner, but he was defeated. It was one of his last losses in a political campaign. The Republican political machine in the Pittsburgh area was publicly damaged as a result of corruption in both city and county offices. In addition, the economic impact of the Great Depression hurt the Republicans nationwide. Lawrence correctly assessed that these conditions created opportunities for his party.

In 1933, President Franklin D. Roosevelt appointed Lawrence to the position of U.S. collector of the Internal Revenue for Western Pennsylvania. The following year, the first Democrat since 1890 was elected governor of Pennsylvania. Governor George Earl promptly made Lawrence the Secretary of the Commonwealth. That same year, 1934, Lawrence became the Democratic State Chairman. He would hold that position until 1945. In 1940, he was elected to the post of Democratic National Committeeman. He would remain in that position until the day he died. It was on April 19, 1942, that he lost his sons in the automobile accident. In an effort to deal with the depression that followed, he concentrated more heavily on his work.

In 1944, the "National Municipal Review" described Pittsburgh as "the dirtiest pile of slag in the United States." The smog in the city was so thick that streetlights often remained on during the daylight hours. The air was unhealthy to breathe, neighborhoods were decaying, the economy was stagnant, and many businesses were looking to leave the city. Faced with these conditions, Lawrence decided to run for mayor. He was elected in 1945, by a margin of approximately 14,000 votes. He would remain in the office for four successive terms. While Lawrence was a dedicated Democrat, he was also a pragmatic administrator who realized that he could not successfully address the city's problems without Republican support. He succeeded in creating bi-partisan coalitions to support a seven point program he proposed called "Renaissance 1" designed to improve the living conditions in Pittsburgh. Among the influential community leaders that Lawrence was able to convince in supporting his programs was Richard K. Mellon. At the time, Mellon was the chairman of one of the largest banks in America and firmly committed to the Republican party.

Under Lawrence's leadership, conditions in Pittsburgh began to change. He formed action groups whose purpose was to address the problem of smog in the city. They succeeded and once that problem had been solved, the city moved forward in other areas. Urban renewal was taking place not only in neighborhoods but in the city's downtown section with the building of skyscrapers. New bridges were built as well as a new airport. The city's universities expanded. There were also new parks, expressways, a new medical center, and a civic and cultural center. In 1957, Fortune magazine named the nine outstanding mayors in the United States. Lawrence was on the list. Pittsburgh received the honor of being named as one of the ten best governed cities in the country.

The Pennsylvania Democratic party clearly wanted to nominate Lawrence as their candidate for governor in 1958. Lawrence, however, had reservations. His age concerned him. He was nearing 70, and he felt he had unfinished work to do in Pittsburgh as mayor. Lawrence was also concerned that his religion would become a factor in the race. He was a Roman Catholic, and the people of Pennsylvania had never elected a Roman Catholic Governor. Finally, he accepted his party's nomination and was successful in overcoming the obstacles he believed he faced. He defeated his Republican opponent by 76,000 votes. Other Democrats didn't fare as well. The outgoing governor George Leader lost a United States Senate race to Hugh Scott. The fact that the outgoing popular Democratic governor, George Leader, lost the United States Senate race illustrates Lawrence's popularity amongst the electorate. In Pennsylvania the General Assembly was split. Democrats controlled the Senate; Republicans, the House. Upon becoming governor, it was clear to Lawrence that he would, once again, need to work with both Democrats and Republicans to accomplish anything.

Lawrence was an active governor. He succeeded in passing stringent highway safety legislation which had the desired results of reducing accidents, injuries, and deaths on Pennsylvania highways. The number of driver suspensions and revocations increased dramatically. One person who lost his license for speeding while Lawrence was governor was his only living son, Jerry, then a college student. He was also successful in passing anti-discrimination legislation and environmental protection laws. He worked to improve tourism, championed and expanded the state's library system, and sought to create new and expanded education programs. In order to balance the state budget, he convinced the legislature to increase the state's sales tax to 4 percent. This angered the state's fiscal conservatives.

In both 1952 and 1956, Lawrence had supported Adlai Stevenson as the Democratic party nominee for president. By 1960, he believed that Democrats needed to move in a new direction and, looking at the candidates, he was strongly attracted to Massachusetts Senator John F. Kennedy. Kennedy was also a Roman Catholic and Lawrence's own success in Pennsylvania may have convinced the pragmatic politician in Lawrence that the country was ready for a Roman Catholic president. At the Democratic convention, Lawrence publicly endorsed Kennedy and the vast majority of Pennsylvania delegates followed his recommendation. Kennedy won the nomination on the first ballot by just 45 votes. Lawrence met with

Final resting place of noted politician and Pennsylvania Governor David Lawrence.

Kennedy and suggested he offer the Vice presidential spot to Senator Lyndon Johnson from Texas. Lawrence believed that a Kennedy-Johnson ticket could unite the party and give the Democrats their best chance of taking back the White House. As it turned out, that was precisely what happened.

Lawrence was limited to one term as governor by Pennsylvania state law. As a result, he left office in 1963. That same year, President Kennedy appointed him to serve as the chairman of the President's Committee on Equal Opportunity in Housing. This was a cause he had committed himself to in his public life so he was a natural choice for the position. He would remain chairman until his death.

In 1966, Pennsylvania Democrats went through a divisive primary to determine the party's nominee for governor. Businessman Milton Shapp (whom the authors would eventually work for) defeated the party's endorsed candidate, State Senator Robert P. Casey, resulting in a weakened Democratic party. Lawrence was determined to do what he could to heal the party divisions. On November 4, 1966, he appeared at a political gathering in Pittsburgh to support Shapp. During his speech, as he appealed for party unity, he collapsed and remained unconscious for seventeen days until he died on November 21, 1966. He was 77 years old.

A Requiem mass was celebrated at Saint Mary's Church where Lawrence had been baptized. The mass was attended by many that had shared the political life with him. His successor, Governor Scranton, was present as was the Governor-Elect Raymond Shafer. President Johnson had sent representatives and numerous mayors of other cities also attended. One mourner arrived unexpectedly. New York Senator Robert F. Kennedy was quickly ushered to the front row and placed closest to the flag draped coffin. David Lawrence is buried in Calvary Cemetery in Pittsburgh.

If You Go:

As always with a cemetery this size the authors strongly encourage you to visit the cemetery office to obtain directions to the grave sites you wish to visit. For more information on who is buried in Calvary see Chapter 6 titled "Half the Horsemen".

15.
"Gone But Not Forgotten"

Lincoln Colored Cemetery
County: Cumberland
Town: Mechanicsburg
Cemetery: Lincoln Colored Cemetery
Address: Winding Hill Road Upper Allen Township

U.S. Colored Infantry during the Civil War.

There are black Civil War Veteran's buried in Mechanicsburg, Pennsylvania in what is called the Lincoln Colored Cemetery. We have lived in Cumberland County for more than 30 years and were astonished to discover that there are black Civil War veterans buried in our county. They

80

are buried in a place called the Lincoln Colored Cemetery in Mechanicsburg, Pennsylvania. If it wasn't for the Boy Scouts of America and Vietnam Veterans of Mechanicsburg, it is very possible that the cemetery would have been forgotten. For a time the Boy Scouts cared for the cemetery. That changed in 1998 when the Vietnam Veterans adopted the cemetery, taking on the responsibility of tending to the grounds. As a result of their efforts, a monument honoring the United States Colored Troops of the Civil War was erected, tombstones were reset, a flag pole flying an American flag and a POW/MIA flag now stands in the cemetery and is illuminated 24 hours every day of the year. Replacement of the flags and a memorial service is held there every Memorial Day at 2:00 pm.

It is difficult to establish many of the facts of how this burial ground came to be and who is buried there. We visited the Cumberland County Historical Society in Carlisle to find out as much as we could. Documents there show that no organization or individual claim ownership of this plot of land. It was, however, an organized colored burial ground and has graves that date as early as 1862. The Vietnam Veterans name twelve veterans of the United States Colored Troops buried there and the Cumberland County Veteran Services Administration lists ten. Research done by Colonel Arthur Cunningham conflicts with both of these claims. Cunningham contributed this research to the website "Lest We Forget". You can visit this site at www.lwfaaf.net. He found two of the soldiers on the Vietnam Veterans' list as buried elsewhere one in Cumberland County and another in Fulton County. This may explain the difference between the Vietnam Veteran's list and the Veteran Services list. The truth will probably never be known but all agree that at least five veterans of the United States Colored Troops are buried there. The five are as follows.

John W. Pinkney was born in 1845 in Frederick Maryland and enlisted at eighteen years of age. He served in Company D, 22nd Regiment United States Colored Troops (USCT). On June 15, 1864 at Petersburg, Virginia he lost the lower part of his left arm to a shell. Amputation was required, and his arm was removed below the shoulder. He died on December 4, 1882.

William Pope was born a slave in Page County Virginia in 1842. He enlisted in Chambersburg, Pennsylvania on February 19, 1964, and served in Company B, 32nd Regiment USCT. He died July 1, 1902.

John Williams was born in Virginia in 1842. He enlisted in Harrisburg on October 13, 1864, and served in Company C, 41st Regiment USCT. He died September 30, 1885, while working in his stable.

Richard "David" Howard, enlisted on June 14, 1864. No birth date or place is known. He served in Company G, 45th Regiment USCT. He was discharged on November 4, 1865. He died September 2, 1895.

William Bridget enlisted on December 30, 1863. He served in Company G, 22nd Regiment USCT. He was discharged on May 24, 1865 and died on September 16, 1900 at the age of 65.

The two that appear to be buried elsewhere are John Berry Sergeant who served with Company C, 5th Regiment Massachusetts Calvary and who is apparently buried in Carlisle, Pennsylvania and James Spriggs who served in Company C, 3rd Regiment USCT is buried in McConnellsburg, PA. Of the remaining five, Ransom Babcock originally enlisted in Company B, 4th Regiment, New York Heavy Artillery, was a Veteran of the Civil War, but may not be buried in the cemetery. Enoch Cook, Reuben Jackson and George Riley could be buried in the cemetery but there is some doubt that they are Civil War Veterans. There is a Henry Butler who is also buried there, but the information on him supplied by the Cumberland County Veterans Services is contested by Colonel Cunningham's research.

Monument marking the entrance to the Lincoln Colored Cemetery.

If You Go:

If you go to Mechanicsburg and visit the Lincoln Colored Cemetery, you might want to visit the Historical Harrisburg Cemetery (see Chapter 5 on Simon Cameron) or the National Civil War Museum in Reservoir Park, Harrisburg.

A few miles from the Lincoln Colored Cemetery is Mount Olivet Cemetery in Fairview Township, near New Cumberland. Mt. Olivet is the final resting place for two Congressional Medal of Honor recipients, John Kirk and George Springer. John Kirk was a 1st Sergeant of Company L, in the United States Calvary during the Indian Wars. He was awarded the Medal of Honor for "Gallantry in action" on July 12, 1870 in the Battle of Little Wichita River.

George Springer was a private in the United States Calvary and was awarded the Medal of Honor also for "Gallantry in action" for action on October 20, 1869 at Chiricahua Mountains, Arizona Territory.

If you go to Mount Olivet there are two great places in New Cumberland for refreshments. Nick's 114 Café on Bridge Street is a very friendly place with excellent food and drinks. It is the place where the authors first discussed the idea for this book. Where the idea itself came from is covered in the Introduction to this volume. Stop in and say hello to Nick's smiling, friendly, attentive staff. You will probably meet Nick himself. Tell him we sent you.

A stone's throw away from Nick's also on Bridge Street is Coakley's Irish Pub. Coakley's also offers fine food and drink with a touch of the Irish. You can utilize the outside patio weather permitting. Coakley's is well known for its St Patrick's Day celebrations. As a matter of fact Saint Patrick's Day week is a continuous party.

16.
"The Tall Tactician"

Connie Mack
County: Philadelphia
Town: Philadelphia
Cemetery: Holy Sepulchre
Address: 3301 Cheltenham Ave

Cornelius McGillicuddy, better known as Connie Mack, was a professional baseball player, manager, and team owner. He played 11 years in the major leagues. As a player he had earned a reputation for being a smart student of the game. However in terms of actual talent, he was considered average at best. It was as a manager where Mack left his mark on the game. He was elected to the Baseball Hall of Fame as a manager in 1937.

Connie Mack was born on December 22, 1862, in East Brookfield, Massachusetts. His parents were Irish immigrants. His father's health had been ruined in the Civil War, and he became an alcoholic who no longer worked. As a result at age 14, after completing the eighth grade, Mack was forced to leave school to help support his family. By the age of 16 he was working in a shoe factory. By age 20 he had been promoted to the position of foreman. When he turned 21 Mack was offered $90 a month to play catcher in the Connecticut State League for Meriden which at that time was a very good salary. He had already acquired the nickname "slats" playing semi-pro ball, and now Meriden shortened his name to "Mack" to fit better on the scorecards.

In 1886, he was signed by the major league Washington D.C. team. In that first season he played in ten games for Washington and had a batting average of .361. In terms of hitting it was the high point of his career. The following season the league instituted a rule change that took away the batter's right to call for a high or low pitch. Word soon spread that Mack couldn't hit the low ball and by 1888, his batting average had fallen to .187. From this point forward it was only his skill as a fielder that allowed him to extend his playing career.

During this time frame Mack made some changes in his personal life. On November 2, 1887, he married Margaret Hogan. They had three children Earle, Roy, and Marguerite. Mack's wife died in 1902 as a result of

Connie Mack

complications that occurred during the birth of the third child.

In 1889, Mack jumped to the Buffalo Bisons of the new (and soon to be defunct) Players League. When the league folded, after one year, he then signed with the Pittsburgh Pirates in 1890. It was in Pittsburgh that Mack ended his playing career in 1896. During his last three years with the Pirates, Mack was the team's player-manager. With his playing career over, he signed on as Manager of the minor league Milwaukee Brewers and managed there for four seasons. It was during his stint in Milwaukee that he would sign the pitching great Rube Waddell, a man who would follow him to the big leagues.

Mack was one of the driving forces behind the creation of a second major league team in Philadelphia. In 1901, he became manager and part owner of the Philadelphia Athletics, a team that would play in the new American League. The league as a whole knew that to survive it would have to field a product that was at least equal to what was being delivered by the already firmly established National League. Mack was up to the challenge. He persuaded Benjamin Shibe, a manufacturer of baseball equipment, to become the president and the club's chief financier. Shibe Park was built to be the new team's home field. Some critics derided the new team as the city's "White Elephant" but Mack turned the insult into a logo, and for decades the team sported white elephants on its uniforms.

Under Mack's leadership the Athletics experienced immediate success. One of his first moves was to sign the hard throwing and aforementioned Rube Waddell. With Rube leading the way, winning 24 games and leading the league in strikeouts, Mack's 1902 Athletics won the American league pennant. They repeated the feat in 1905 and appeared in the first World Series. Mack's team faced John McGraw's New Giants in that initial series. With Waddell unable to pitch due a shoulder injury, the Giant's Christy Mathewson dominated the series winning three games and leading his team to the championship four games to one.

Mack's style of managing, which was described as intelligent and innovative, earned him another nickname: the Tall Tactician. He valued intelligence in his players and wanted them to be self-disciplined. Unfortunately for Mack, Rube Waddell turned out to be a character. Rube was anything but self-disciplined. He developed a habit of exiting the stadium during games to follow fire trucks. In the off-season he found employment as an alligator wrestler. On the mound he was distracted by opposing fans that would hold up shiny objects. When they caught his attention, it seemed as if he was in a trance. Waddell also had a drinking problem severe enough that the Sporting News called him "sousepaw". By early 1908, Mack could take no more, and he traded Rube to Saint Louis. Waddell was a tremendous talent as evidenced by the fact that he won six consecutive American League strikeout titles. He was unable, however, to deal with his personal demons. He died in 1914 in a sanitarium in Texas. Waddell was elected to the Baseball Hall of Fame in 1946.

In 1910, Mack married Katherine Hallahan. It was his second marriage. It appears to have been a success for the whole family. His sons from his previous marriage would become executives with the Athletics. His team would become a family business. Connie Mack was determined to remain as head of the family.

The Philadelphia Athletics won their first World Series for Mack in 1910. Mack's team repeated the feat in 1911, beating the Giants and getting revenge at the expense of John McGraw. Mack's team at the time included the future Hall of famers Eddie Collins and Frank "Home Run" Baker. Mack led the Athletics to a third World Championship in 1913. He had them back in the series the following year, but the Athletics were upset by the Boston Braves.

Starting in 1916, Mack's teams hit hard times. For seven consecutive seasons the Athletics finished in last place. It's hard to believe a manager could survive a showing like that today, but being an owner of the team probably helped. Mack remained at the helm and in the mid-1920's, the Athletics were once again competing for league titles.

During this time Mack recruited and developed some great players including catcher Mickey Cochrane (Mickey Mantle was named after Cochrane). Mack also signed the great pitcher Lefty Grove, and the power hitting outfielder Jimmie Fox. All three players were elected to the Baseball Hall Fame. From 1925 to 1933, the Athletics finished in third place twice, they were the runner-up four times and they won three American League titles. In 1929, they won another World Series and then repeated in 1930. They made it to the series in 1931 but were defeated. As the Great Depression worsened, attendance fell sharply and Mack was forced to sell his best players. While he would manage until 1950, he would not win another championship.

At the time of his retirement in 1950 he was 87 years old. His 50 year tenure is the most for a coach or manager with the same team in North American professional sports. He won nine pennants and appeared in eight World Series, winning five. Even during his dark final years his popularity not only endured but it grew. George M. Cohan (of Yankee Doddle Dandy fame) wrote a song about him. In 1944, he was voted favorite manager in the game by players and sportswriters. He never wore a uniform while managing, always wearing a suit. Fans came to games just to see him. By this time he was almost regarded as a holy relic by the game of baseball.

After he retired as manager, he remained owner and president, although his sons increasingly took over the running of the team. He remained president until 1954. He holds the records for both most wins and most losses. However no other manager has managed to get within 1,000 wins of his total. Mack resigned as president of the Athletics after the 1954 season. When he stepped down he sold the team to Arnold Johnson, who moved the Athletics to Kansas City.

Even after leaving the game, more honors continued to come Mack's way. Shibe Park was renamed Connie Mack Stadium in 1953. In addition to his Hall Of Fame election, he was the first person inducted into the New York City based Irish American Baseball Hall Of Fame. He is also mentioned in Ogden Nash's poem "Line-up For Yesterday".

Connie Mack died on February 8, 1956. He was 94 years old. The

The grave of one of baseball's greatest men and minds makes no mention of his contributions to the nation's national past time.

priest at his funeral said, "It is not the custom in our church at requiem mass to preach a sermon." However according to the great sportswriter Red Smith (a close friend of Mack's) Father Cartin made an exception. He said, "Those who know the greatness of this man can pay tribute to his greatness far better than I... His memory is held sacred in the lives of our people in general, whose inspiration he was... He will indeed be missed by our American people, generations young and old." He is buried in Holy Sepulchre Cemetery in Cheltenham, PA. His grave says simply "McGillicuddy". There is no indication of his first name or any of his accomplishments.

If You Go:

Holy Sepulchre is a beautiful, well maintained cemetery with a number of noteworthy graves. Frank Rizzo, the controversial Police Commissioner and Mayor of Philadelphia, is buried there. (See Chapter 25).

Another interesting story is that of Billy Maharg whose real name was Graham or Maharg spelled backwards. Maharg had a strange Major League baseball history which consisted of appearing in two games, one game and one at-bat in each league. He appeared in 1912 as a replacement player for the Detroit Tigers when a group of Tigers refused to play as a protest to Ty Cobbs suspension for attacking a fan in the stands. The replacement Tigers lost to the Philadelphia Athletics 24-2. Maharg went 0 for 1 in that game and then played again in 1916 for the Phillies when he was given the chance

Here lies Billy Maherg (Graham spelled backwards) who was a main player in the 1919 world series scandal.

to bat in the final game of the season. He was employed by the Phillies as a driver and assistant trainer. He is best known, however, for his role in the infamous Black Sox scandal of 1919. Maharg conspired with eight players to fix the World Series in exchange for $100,000. Maharg and his partner in crime, Sleepy Bill Burns, approached New York gambler Arnold Rothstein to make a deal. Other gamblers got involved and Maharg and Burns suffered multiple double-crosses. A disgruntled Maharg gave the full details to a Philadelphia writer in 1920, and eight players were indicted. Maharg testified in the trial and the players were found not guilty but were banned from baseball for life. Actor Richard Edson played Maharg in the 1988 film "Eight Men Out".

Also buried nearby is John H. McVeigh, a World War II Congressional Medal of Honor recipient. He was an infantry Sergeant who was awarded the CMOH for his bravery near Brest, France on August 29, 1944. In a savage hand-to-hand struggle with German troops, he was shot and killed at point blank range.

Holy Sepulchre also contains the grave of William "Bill" Hewitt, a Hall of Fame professional football player. Hewitt played for the Bears and Eagles in the 1930's.

Finally, if you visit Holy Sepulchre, you are about one mile away from the Ivy Hill Cemetery. For information on who you can visit at Ivy Hill see Chapter 1 on Willie Anderson.

17.
"The Blond Bombshell"

Jayne Mansfield
County: Northampton
Town: Pen Argyl
Cemetery: Fairview Cemetery
Address: South Main Street - Pen Argyl

Jayne Mansfield was an American actress who worked on both the Broadway stage and in Hollywood movies. She was born on April 19, 1933 in Bryn Mawr, Pennsylvania. Her name at birth was Vera Jayne Palmer. Early in her childhood, her family moved to Dallas, Texas. It was in Dallas that she spent her formative years. She studied at the University of Dallas and the University of Texas. She spoke five languages and reportedly had a very high IQ. She claimed it was 163. In addition, she was classically trained on both the piano and violin.

While in Dallas, she began to study acting. She was a student of Baruch Lumet, the father of the famed Hollywood director Sidney Lumet. She was also busy winning beauty contests having been named "Miss Photoflash", "Miss Fire Prevention Week," and "Miss Magnesium Lamp."

In the early 1950's, she was working at the Pasadena Playhouse. A Warner Brothers talent scout discovered her and signed her to a contract. Her movie career began with bit parts. Her appearance in movies and her pictorial as the Playboy Playmate of the month in February 1955 turned her into one of the leading sex symbols of her era.

Mansfield's first movie role was in "Female Jungle," a 1954 production. She appeared in a film starring Jack Webb Titled "Pete Kelly's Blues" in 1955. That same year, she returned to Broadway, appearing in the successful play "Will Success Spoil Rock Hunter?" By the next year, she was back in Hollywood starring in "The Girl Can't Help It." This film included performances from early rock stars such as Eddie Cochrane, Fats Domino, and Little Richard. I think we can all agree that a meeting between Mansfield and Little Richard would have been worth seeing.

In 1957, she reprised her Broadway role for the film "Will Success Spoil Rock Hunter?" The film was a success. As a matter of fact, "The Girl Can't Help It" and "Will Success..." are now considered classics. That same year she appeared in the film "The Wayward Bus" with Dan Dailey and Joan Collins. For her performance, she earned the Golden Globe award as New

Actress Jayne Mansfield

Star of the Year in the actress category. Natalie Wood was among the other nominees. Unfortunately for Mansfield, she also appeared in "Kiss Them for Me" with Gary Grant that same year. The film was soundly panned by the critics and, as it turned out, was her final starring role for a well known Hollywood studio.

After that, quality roles in quality films were not offered to Mansfield. In 1963, she appeared in "Promises, Promises" where she became the first well known mainstream American actress to appear nude on film. The city of Cleveland banned the movie, though it did enjoy box office success elsewhere.

Though her Hollywood career was floundering she continued to have success in other venues. She appeared on stage in Vegas in a show titled "The House of Love." For her efforts there, she earned $35,000 per week. Even without making films, she was earning anywhere from $8,000 to $25,000 a week for her night club act. She also made a few recordings. In 1965 she released, "As the Clouds Drift By" with "Suey" on the flip side. One of the backing musicians on the recordings was Jimi Hendrix.

At that point in her career, she was also doing television variety shows. She did the popular Ed Sullivan Show and also appeared with Jack Benny, Steve Allen, and Jackie Gleason. She entertained the troops with Bob Hope when he did his tours entertaining the boys overseas. While her film career was over, she was making a great living in the entertainment business.

Mansfield was married three times. Two of her marriages ended in divorce. There were rumors of numerous sexual affairs that included liaisons with men such as John F. Kennedy. She was the mother of five children. One of her children, Mariska Hargitay, is known for her role in the television series "Law and Order: Special Victims Unit".

On June 28, 1967, Mansfield was performing in Biloxi, Mississippi at the Gus Stevens Supper Club. After the performance, she, a male friend, their driver Ronnie Harrison, and three of Mansfield's children who were in the back seat, headed for New Orleans. The party needed to get there that night because Mansfield was scheduled to do a television interview the following morning. At about 2:25 a.m. on June 29th the car carrying Mansfield and her passengers crashed into the rear of a tractor trailer. All three adults died instantly; the children escaped with minor injuries. Word spread that Mansfield had been decapitated. This was untrue; she died from fatal head trauma.

Jayne Mansfield is buried beneath a beautiful heart shaped headstone in Fairview Cemetery in Pen Argyl Pennsylvania. As evidenced by the grave goods (in her case coins) we found on her tombstone, Mansfield has not been forgotten. In 1980 the "Jayne Mansfield Story" aired on CBS. It starred Loni Anderson and Arnold Schwarzenegger. It was nominated for three Emmy awards.

If You Go:

While there are no other cemeteries of note in the vicinity of Fairview, you are within a half hour of Allentown. Right in downtown Allentown, behind the old Pennsylvania Power and Light building (you can't miss it as

The sex symbol form the 50's and 60's lies beneath this beautiful tombstone. Note the grave goods (coins) left for her after all these years. Some guys never forget.

Veterans of the American Revolution and the War of 1812 lie in this old Allentown cemetery.

it is by far the tallest structure in the city) lies an old cemetery. Within this cemetery lie the remains of many veterans of the American Revolution and the War of 1812.

The authors admit they were perplexed as to how Jayne Mansfield came to be buried in Pen Argyl. As it turns out, we stopped to have lunch in a small diner just outside of Pen Argyl in the town of Gap. We quizzed our waitress but she had no idea who Jayne Mansfield was. She did tell us that there was a gentleman named Charlie in the diner who knew all the local history, and she offered to direct him to our table. We immediately accepted the offer.

Charlie arrived in a flash. We later guessed him to be in his late 70's or early 80's, but he was still in great physical condition, and he appeared to be sharp as a tack. After introducing ourselves we asked about Mansfield. Charlie advised us that Mansfield's mother had settled in Pen Argyl and that she had arranged to have the body shipped there for burial. He also said that Mansfield had other relatives in the area. He then told us he used to have drinks with one of her cousins all the time at the local Legion, until he (Charlie) was banned from the club due to his fondness for foul language.

Charlie asked us why we were interested in Jayne Mansfield and we explained the basis of the book to him. He immediately said, "You boys are doing Mary Jo Kopechne, right?" We had to admit she wasn't on our list, but agreed she should be (See Chapter 13). Our thanks go out to Charlie for the information on Mansfield and for bringing Mary Jo to our attention.

18.
"A Harrisburg Hero"

Vance Criswell McCormick
County: Dauphin
Town: Harrisburg
Cemetery: Harrisburg Cemetery
Address: 521 North 13th Street

Vance McCormick was a man who seemed to meet with success in anything to which he devoted himself. As a youth he was a tremendous athlete. He did well in school on every level. He found success in the publishing business. McCormick also ran numerous family businesses after the death of his father. He tried his hand at politics and made a name for himself there as well. He became the good friend of a president whom he served ably in negotiating the peace after World War 1.

McCormick was born on June 19, 1872, in the vicinity of Harrisburg Pennsylvania. His father, Henry McCormick, was well known and wealthy. He served the Union during the Civil War, and when the war ended, became a successful businessman and civic leader. He was part of a group that founded the Harrisburg Hospital. The Harrisburg area held Henry McCormick in very high esteem. Their respect for him was evidenced when the community chose to have him lead the funeral procession for Abraham Lincoln when the murdered president's body was brought to Harrisburg to lie in state.

Henry McCormick saw to it that his son was well educated. Vance McCormick attended a prestigious private school, Harrisburg Academy, which is still in operation today. Prior to college, he also attended Phillips Andover, a private boarding school located about 25 miles north of Boston, Massachusetts. The graduates of this school include the inventor Samuel Morse, four Medal of Honor recipients, the author Oliver Wendell Holmes, Sr., NFL Head Coach Bill Belichick, and two presidents George H. and George W. Bush. When it was time to make a college choice there was little doubt about the selection McCormick would make. His father was a Yale man, as was his uncle, brother, and six of his cousins. McCormick, of course, followed the family tradition.

It was at Yale where McCormick exhibited his abundant athletic talents. He was named captain of his class football and baseball teams

Vance McCormick with Woodrow Wilson

during his first two years at the university. In his junior and senior years, he continued participation in both sports as a member of the Yale varsity teams. During McCormick's senior year the football team went undefeated and unscored upon in 13 games. His success on the football field is documented by the fact that after his senior year he was named to Walter Camp's All-American squad as the first team quarterback. After graduation he assisted in establishing the first football team at the Carlisle Indian School. A fellow by the name of Jim Thorpe would put that school on the national football stage a few years later.

McCormick graduated from Yale in 1893, and he was awarded an honorary MA degree by the university in 1907. After graduation, McCormick returned to the Harrisburg area and went into business with his father. In 1900, Henry McCormick passed away and McCormick became the trustee of the estates of his father and uncle. This brought him into the business world as the estates were involved in farming, coal and mining properties, railroads, and timberlands. In addition to being the President of the Pinkey Mining Company, it was at this time that McCormick entered the publishing business. He became President of the Patriot Company, which published the Harrisburg area's important newspapers including *The Patriot* which he led from 1902 to 1946, and the Evening News which he founded in 1917 and ran until 1946.

During these busy times McCormick was also a public servant. In 1902 he was elected Mayor of Harrisburg. He immediately set out to improve the living conditions within the city. He expanded the city park system and built steps along the Susquehanna River. Those steps are still in existence today. He was responsible for the paving of seventy miles of roads. In addition, he improved the city water system. While he was mayor, the population of Harrisburg grew from 51,000 to 73,000.

In 1914, McCormick was nominated by the Democratic Party as its candidate for Governor of Pennsylvania. He was defeated in the general election. Two years later he was appointed chairman of the Democratic National Committee, a position he held until 1919. It was during this time that he became friends with President Woodrow Wilson. At the conclusion of World War 1, in 1919, Wilson selected McCormick to chair the American Commission to Negotiate Peace at Versailles. While he carried out his duties, in terms of serving the president, McCormick was troubled by the finished treaty. It was his view that the British insistence on punishing the Germans (particularly the amount of reparations Germany was required to pay) was a mistake. Because of this view, McCormick may be considered somewhat of a prophet since many believe that the seeds of World War 2 were planted within the treaty that emerged from Versailles.

While he never held an elected office again, he remained active in

Side View of the McCormick Mausoleum located in Harrisburg.

public service throughout his life. Through the years he was appointed to numerous local, state, national and international organizations. At the same time he remained active in managing his business concerns.

Vance McCormick did not marry until he was 52 years old. He and his wife had no children of their own. We discovered that McCormick did, however, have an interest in children. We met a man, who is now in his eighties, who says that McCormick took a liking to him when he was a boy. According to this gentleman, who described himself as a poor farm boy, McCormick obtained permission from his mother to pick up the youngster and take him to the McCormick estate where he enjoyed meals and the use of the swimming pool. He also says that McCormick would treat him to ice cream and candy. The man doesn't have one bad thing to say about Vance McCormick.

McCormick passed away at his country estate, in the vicinity of Cedar Cliff Farms, on June 16, 1946. He died three days shy of his 74th birthday. He was laid to rest with his father in the McCormick mausoleum in the Harrisburg Cemetery.

If You Go:

See the "If You Go" section in Chapter 5 on Simon Cameron. In addition to the comments in Chapter 5, the Firehouse Restaurant on 2nd Street in Harrisburg is a great place to relax and unwind. Stop in for a Mojito, the signature drink, meet their friendly staff, and check out the menu. The Firehouse itself is a bit of history which you can explore and enjoy while you replenish your vital fluids and partake of some nourishment.

19.
"The Old Snapping Turtle"

George Meade
County: Philadelphia
Town: Philadelphia
Cemetery: Laurel Hill Cemetery
Address: 3822 Ridge Avenue

George Gordon Meade was a career United States Army officer and is best known for being the victor of the Battle of Gettysburg in 1863. He was born on December 31, 1815, in Spain. His father was serving there as an agent for the United States Government. In 1828, his father died and six months later the family, facing financial difficulties, returned to the United States. Initially George was educated at the Mount Hope Institution in Baltimore. In 1831, with financial considerations being a prime consideration, he entered the United States Military Academy at West Point. He graduated ranked nineteenth in his class of 56 cadets in 1835 and was transferred to Florida at the beginning of the Seminole Wars. He became ill with a fever in Florida and was reassigned to Massachusetts. He was very disillusioned with the military and resigned his commission in 1836. He went to work for a railroad company as an engineer to survey territory for new rail lines.

In 1840 he met Margaretta Sergeant and soon she became his wife. She was the daughter of John Sergeant who was Henry Clay's running mate in the 1832 presidential election. They had seven children together. With a family to support, Meade found it difficult to secure steady employment. Though he had never intended to make the army a career, he reapplied to the military in 1842 and was appointed a 2nd Lieutenant in the Topographical Engineers. He was assigned to General Winfield Scott's Army during the War with Mexico. He was brevetted to first lieutenant as a result of his conduct during the Battle of Monterrey.

After the war in Mexico was over, Meade moved back to Philadelphia where he worked on building lighthouses for the Delaware Bay. He was eventually promoted to Captain, and for the next ten years he spent time in surveying and design work for lighthouses on the east coast. He oversaw the construction of lighthouses at Barnegat, Atlantic City, and Cape May, New Jersey. Among his accomplishments during this period was the design of a hydraulic lamp that was approved by the Lighthouse Board for use in

George Gordon Meade

American lighthouses. He also participated in the survey of the Great Lakes and tributaries.

He was promoted from Captain to Brigadier General in August 1861, just a few months after the start of the Civil War. The sectional strife took a personal toll on the Meades as his wife's sister was married to Governor Wise of Virginia who became a Brigadier General in the Confederate Army. Nicknamed "The Old Snapping Turtle", Meade gained a reputation for being short- tempered and obstinate. In March 1862, he was severely wounded at the Battle of Glendale. A musket ball struck him above his hip, clipped his liver, and just missed his spine as it passed through his body. He recovered from his wounds in Philadelphia and led his brigade at the Battle of Second Bull Run and at the Battles of South Mountain, Antietam, and Fredericksburg. Soon after Fredericksburg, Meade was assigned to command the Fifth Army Corps of the Army of the Potomac. His assignment as corps commander took him through the trial of the Battle of Chancellorsville in May 1863. Though the army had been soundly defeated there, Meade handled his corps with great skill and protected the important fords on the Rappahannock River.

Unhappy with the performance of the Army of the Potomac, President Lincoln changed command from McClellan to Burnside to Hooker to Meade. Meade assumed command just days before the monumental Battle of Gettysburg, which is considered the turning point of the War. Meade was not Lincoln's first choice as he asked John Reynolds to take command but Reynolds declined. In defending his decision to appoint Meade as commander of the union forces, Lincoln said, "Meade will fight well on his own dunghill."

Meade was fortunate to have such competent and brave officers as Reynolds, Buford, Hancock, Vincent, Custer, and Chamberlain with him at Gettysburg. Meade made the decision to fight a defensive battle and did well in deploying his forces. His forces repelled attacks on his flanks and on the final day of the battle, stood tall against an attack on the center of their lines. This disastrous attack became known as Pickett's Charge. Although Meade field-marshaled the Union victory at Gettysburg, he was criticized severely then and now for not pursuing the defeated Confederate forces after the battle. Meade infuriated Lincoln when he reported that the "invaders have been driven from our land." Reportedly, upon receiving the dispatch, Lincoln said angrily "Doesn't he understand it's all our land?" Lincoln was overwrought at the missed opportunity to perhaps end the war and ordered Meade to pursue and attack Lee's retreating Army. It was too late however, and Lee escaped to Virginia. In March, Lincoln put General Ulysses S. Grant in charge of all Union Armies.

General Meade's monument at Gettysburg.

When Grant was appointed, Meade offered his resignation. He wanted to give Grant the opportunity to appoint the general of his choosing for the position. Grant told Meade he had no intention of replacing him. While

105

Meade stayed with the Army, he did not approve of Grant's tactics. Meade had become a cautious general while Grant was willing to attack and suffer losses, secure in the knowledge that he had replacements available and the confederates did not. By all accounts, Meade served Grant well during the remainder of the war. He received a promotion to Major General at the war's end. He was outranked by only Grant, Halleck, and Sherman.

After the War, General Meade was a Commissioner of Fairmont Park

Final resting place of George Meade (the old snapping turtle) who commanded the victorious Union Army at Gettysburg.

Tombstone of Ulric Dahlgren, who was killed in a raid on Richmond, while carrying orders to assassinate Confederate President Jefferson Davis.

in Philadelphia from 1866 until his death. Prior to his death he received an honorary doctorate in law from Harvard University. In addition, his scientific achievements were recognized by several institutions, including the American Philosophical Society and The Philadelphia Academy of Natural Sciences. He died on November 6, 1872 in the house where he lived at 1836 Delancey Place in Philadelphia from complications of his old wounds combined with pneumonia. He was 56 years old. Many felt his victory at Gettysburg had stopped a rebel invasion of the city. After his death, his widow accepted the house as a gift from the city of Philadelphia. To this day the house still has the word "Meade" over the door though now it has been converted into apartments. Meade is buried in a modest grave in Laurel Hill Cemetery in Philadelphia.

If You Go:

Laurel Hill is a large well- kept cemetery rich in history with many interesting graves. (See chapter 12 on Harry Kalas). Once again due to the size of this cemetery if you visit, we advise you to make an initial stop at the cemetery office to obtain directions to the sites you are there to see.

Among the graves at Laurel Hill are three officers who fought with Meade at Gettysburg. Oliver Blatchy Knowles entered the war as a private and ended it as Brevet Brigadier General after fighting in Antietam, Shenandoah, Gettysburg, Spotsylvania, Petersburg and the last campaign of Appomattox. He died less than two years after the war of cholera at the age of 25. William Lovering Curry fought at Gettysburg and was stationed at the famed "Copse of Trees" during Picketts' Charge. He was wounded at the Battle of Spotsylvania and died a month later. Alexander Williams Biddle fought at the Battles of Fredericksburg, Chancellorsville, Gettysburg, and Bristoe Station as a Major and then Lieutenant Colonel.

Ulric Dahlgren was a Civil War army officer killed in a raid on Richmond in 1864. Papers found on him indicated he had orders to assassinate Confederate President Jefferson Davis (the Dahlgren Affair) and his Cabinet. The papers were published and created an enormous controversy in the following months and may have contributed to John Wilkes Booth's decision to assassinate Abraham Lincoln a year later.

Frank Furness served as a Civil War officer and was awarded the Congressional Medal of Honor for his bravery at Trevailian Station Virginia. However he was better known as a major architect from 1870 to 1890. He designed over 400 buildings including banks, churches, synagogues, rail stations and numerous mansions. His first major work, Philadelphia's Academy of Fine Arts, is still standing. His grave, however, is very modest and simple.

There are five other Civil War Congressional Medal of Honor Recipients at Laurel Hill: Henry Harrison Bingham, George J. Pitman, John Hamilton Storey, Pinkerton Vaughn, and Robert Teleford Kelly.

20.
"A Pennsylvania Patriot"

Thomas Mifflin
County: Lancaster
Town: Lancaster
Cemetery: Trinity Lutheran Church
Address: 31 South Duke St.

Thomas Mifflin is one of the Founding Fathers of our country. He risked his life for American Independence and democracy. He spent almost his entire life in public service. He was expelled from his church for fighting the British, was a signer of the U.S. Constitution, and was Pennsylvania's first governor. Despite his many accomplishments and his contributions as a founding father, there is no monument that identifies his grave. There is a historical marker saying he is interred somewhere on the grounds of Trinity Lutheran Church. It is uncertain where precisely he is buried. In addition, there is little mention of his many distinguished accomplishments during his long life of service to his country and his state. One internet site claims the grave was paved over for a parking lot. There is a marble slab in the wall of the church that states he was a signer of the Constitution.

Thomas Mifflin was born on January 10, 1744, in Philadelphia where his parents were prominent Quakers. He attended local schools and in 1760, graduated from the College of Philadelphia (today known as the University of Pennsylvania). He went into business with a local merchant and in 1765, he formed a partnership in the import and export business with his younger brother.

Mifflin married a distant cousin, Sarah Morris, in 1771. That same year, he was elected city warden. In 1772, he began the first of four consecutive terms in the Colonial legislature. In the summer of 1774, Mifflin was elected by the legislature to the First Continental Congress. His work there spread his reputation across America and led to his election to the Second Continental Congress which convened in Philadelphia in the aftermath of the fighting at Lexington and Concord.

He played a major role in the creation of Philadelphia's militia and was commissioned as a Major. Although his family were Quakers for generations, he was expelled from the church because military service violated the pacifist nature of the faith.

When Congress created the Continental Army in June 1775, Mifflin

Thomas Mifflin

resigned from Congress in order to go on active duty with the regulars. George Washington, the Commander in Chief of the Army, selected Mifflin as one of his aides. Shortly after, Washington appointed him Quartermaster General of the Continental Army. His service as Quartermaster earned him a promotion to Brigadier General, but he longed for a field command and requested to be reassigned. He was transferred to the infantry and led a brigade of Pennsylvania continentals during the New York City campaign. However, he was soon returned to the position of Quartermaster when no suitable replacement could be found for him. It was a move that left him bitterly disappointed.

In November 1776, General Mifflin was sent by Washington to Philadelphia to report to the Continental Congress the critical condition of the army. The Continental Army was outgunned and outmanned and unable to make a stand in New Jersey to stop the advancing British march towards Philadelphia. It was a wise move by the Commander-in-Chief to send General Mifflin to rally Philadelphia, as Congress, in fear of losing the Capital was preparing to take flight to Baltimore. When the Continental army was forced into Pennsylvania, the citizens of Philadelphia began to panic. Business was suspended, schools were closed, and roads leading from the city were crowded with refugees all fleeing the city. (Sort of like rush hour on today's Schuykill Expressway).

At a town meeting, General Mifflin addressed the crowd and much of the Continental Congress. After listening to Mifflin, Congress formally appealed to the militia of Philadelphia and surrounding areas to join Washington's army. Mifflin organized and trained three regiments of militia and sent 1,500 men to Washington. He also orchestrated a re-supply of Washington's desperate troops once they reached Valley Forge. These were critical components needed by Washington to cross the Delaware and attack the British in Trenton. In recognition of his services, Congress commissioned Mifflin as a major-general and made him a member of the Board of War.

On the Board of War, General Mifflin joined a growing number of delegates and generals who shared the dissatisfaction of General Washington's conduct of the war. He sympathized with the views of General Horatio Gates and General Thomas Conway who blamed Washington for the losses of the Continental Army. In the fall of 1777, Horatio Gates, with the help of Benedict Arnold, defeated the British forces at Saratoga. Almost immediately, Washington's enemies, emboldened by the victory, sought his replacement with the "Hero of Saratoga" General Gates. General Conway organized an effort to have the Board of War establish Gates as the new Commander in Chief. This became known as "The Conway Cabal". When the effort failed, Mifflin submitted his resignation. Congress refused to accept it,

Historical marker noting the burial site of Thomas Mifflin.

Plaque marking possible gravesite of Thomas Mifflin.

but he was discharged from the Board of War.

In late 1778, while still on active duty, he won reelection to the State Legislature. In 1780, he was again elected to the Continental Congress and in 1783, the Continental Congress elected him as President of the Congress. He presided over the ratification of the Treaty of Paris, which ended the Revolution and ironically accepted Washington's formal resignation as Commander in Chief. In what many historians say was one of the most remarkable events of United States history George Washington was formally received by President Thomas Mifflin and Congress. At the pinnacle of his power and popularity, Washington resigned his commission as Commander in Chief to the President of The Continental Congress, a man who had once conspired to replace him.

He represented Pennsylvania at the United States Constitutional Convention and was a signer of it. He presided over the committee that wrote Pennsylvania's first constitution which established a bicameral legislature with a strong governor. He then ran for governor in 1790, and was elected as Pennsylvania's first governor by a margin of almost ten to one. He served three terms as governor until 1799.

Thomas Mifflin died on January 20, 1800, in Lancaster and was buried in the cemetery of Trinity Lutheran Church at state expense since his estate was too small to cover funeral costs. The cemetery no longer exists. Most of the bodies were moved in the 1840's to Woodward Hill Cemetery, but Mifflin's was not. There is a historical marker on South Duke Street that says "here interred the remains of Thomas Wharton Jr. and Governor Thomas Mifflin".

If You Go:

Right around the corner from the meager marker for Thomas Mifflin on East King Street is Annie Bailey's Irish Pub. We went there to have a pint while we contemplated the travesty we had just seen. While there, we were impressed with the food, the service, and the fine original Irish craftsmanship that went into the whole first floor. As a matter of fact, we were informed that the bar itself had been transported to Lancaster from a pub in Ireland.

21.
"The Molly Maguires"

The Molly Maguires
Black Jack Kehoe and Franklin Gowen
Counties: Schuylkill and Philadelphia
Towns: Tamaqua and Philadelphia
Cemetery: Kehoe - Old Saint Jerome's Cemetery
Address: Corner of High and Nescopeck Streets, Tamaqua
Cemetery: Gowen - Ivy Hill Cemetery
Address: 1201 Easton Road, Philadelphia

In Pennsylvanian history, there are few groups as interesting or as controversial as the Molly Maguires. Some historians view them as an Irish Catholic terrorist organization, while to others, they are no more than an organized labor movement created as a response to the persecution of Irish coal miners. Still, there are some who argue that the organization never existed. Undeniable, however, is the fact is that between June 21, 1877, and October 9, 1879, twenty Irish catholic men were hanged for murder and accused of belonging to a secret society known as the Molly Maguires. Ten of these men were hanged on June 21, 1877, a day that would become known as "Black Thursday" or "The Day of the Rope".

The Molly Maguire story began in the early 1860's and ended in 1879 when the last hanging took place. The center of action was the anthracite coal region in northeastern Pennsylvania. The alleged Mollies were most active in two counties Carbon and Schuylkill.

As a result of the potato famine in the late 1840's, many Irish immigrates landed in America. Those who settled in the Pennsylvania coal region found that the only jobs available to them were in the mines. The work was difficult and dangerous. In addition, the miners were forced to live in coal company provided housing and could only shop at the company store where prices were so inflated that it was not unusual for a miner to find himself in debt to the company as his wages could not cover his rent and other expenses. These conditions led to the beatings and murder of mine owners, foreman and superintendents. The mine owners and newspapers believed these beatings and killings were part of an organized conspiracy headed by Irishmen who called themselves the Molly Maguires.

During the Molly era, the miners were forming a union under the

John "Black Jack" Kehoe, "King of the Mollies," soon before his execution in 1878.

leadership of John Siney. The union was known as the Workingmen's Benevolent Association and through Siney, and the leadership of the organization as a whole, they sought to seek concessions through negotiations. At times, they used strikes as a tool. In December of 1874, what was called the long strike began in the coalfields. The strike lasted for just under six months and when the miners broke they were forced to return for lower wages than they had previously earned. The person responsible for this settlement was Franklin B. Gowen, the President of the Philadelphia and Reading Coal and Iron Company.

Gowen was born in Mount Airy, Pennsylvania on February 9, 1836. He was the fifth child of an Irish Protestant immigrant who made his living as a grocer. Franklin attended a boarding school, John Beck's Boys Academy, starting at age 9 and ending when he was 13. After serving an apprenticeship to a Lancaster merchant, he decided to study law and worked under an attorney in Pottsville, Pennsylvania which happened to be the county seat of Schuylkill County. In 1860 he was admitted to the County Bar and in 1862 he was elected District Attorney of Schuylkill County. He held this position until 1864 when he resigned in order to pursue a private practice. Among his clients was the Philadelphia and Reading Railroad. He soon left private practice to head that company's legal department. It proved to be a wise move for in 1869, Gowen was appointed acting President of the company.

By this time, Gowen already had the Molly Maguires in his sights. In 1873, he hired the Pinkerton Detective Agency for the purpose of infiltrating the Mollies. Several Pinkerton operatives were sent into the coalfields, including James McParlan, who arrived in Schuylkill County on October 27,1873, using the alias of James McKenna. In April of 1874, McParlan was initiated into the Ancient Order of Hibernians (AOH), a legal Irish Catholic organization. It was Gowen's belief that the Molly Maguires operated within this organization. It is worth noting that violence on both management's and labor's side increased once the Pinkertons arrived in the area.

The Pinkertons were not the only weapon used by Gowen in his attacks on the Mollies. He had his own private police force known as the Coal and Iron police. An 1868 act of the legislature authorized the creation of this private army. A deputy commissioner for Pennsylvania's Bureau of Labor Statistics held the opinion that the coal operators were their own personal government in the middle of a republic. There was no limit to the number of Coal and Iron policemen that could be hired by the Reading Coal and Iron Company, nor were there any background checks on those who applied to join the force. This police force patrolled the coal region unmolested by local authorities. In May of 1875, Pinkerton sent Captain Robert Linden to the coal fields. He immediately received an appointment as

The tombstones in this old cemetery have been destroyed due to vandalism. Two alleged Molly Maguires are buried here including Alec Campbell. Almost all historians agree that one of the two interned here, placed their handprint on his cell wall prior to his execution. The print remains to this day as a sign of his innocence.

a Coal and Iron policeman. The power of this police force was absolute. They were more powerful than the civil authorities. Linden was instrumental in investigating the crimes that led to the arrests of the alleged Molly Maguires.

One of the most important murders in the Molly Maguire story took place in Tamaqua during the evening hours on July 5, 1875. The Tamaqua police force consisted of two men: Barney McCarron and Benjamin Yost. Yost had a history of running into trouble with an Irish minor named James Kerrigan. Yost had arrested Kerrigan on several occasions for public drunkenness, and in at least one instance subdued Kerrigan with his billy club.

One of the duties of the Tamaqua police force was to extinguish the gas street lights. As Yost was climbing a ladder to shut off one of the light, shots rang out, and Yost fell to the ground. McCarron Turned towards the sound of the shots and saw two forms running away. McCarron gave chase but the assailants escaped. Yost died several hours later and word spread that the murder had been carried out by the Molly Maguires.

The first Mollies that ended up on the gallows were arrested in September of 1875 for the murder of mine superintendent John P. Jones. Jones was shot and killed at a railroad station in Lansford while on his way to work by two men who quickly left the scene. A witness to the murder quickly made the trip to Tamaqua and spread the news. In addition, this man claimed to have seen a man waving something white in the woods outside Tamaqua an apparent signal that brought two other men to him. A posse was formed to investigate. The three men arrested for the crime were found in those same woods having a meal. The men were identified as Edward Kelly, Michael Doyle, and Jimmy Kerrigan. Both Kelly and Doyle carried documents that identified them as members of the AOH. The three were taken to the Carbon County jail in Mauch Chunk, now known as Jim Thorpe.

These initial arrests provided the break the Pinkertons were waiting for, and they quickly took advantage of it. The accused men requested separate trials, and Michael Doyle was the first to be tried. Meanwhile Kerrigan and Kelly were kept in solitary confinement in the county jail.

This initial trial set the tone for the ones that would follow. The jury would have no Irish or catholic members and would be made up largely of Germans, including some who spoke little or no English. The District Attorney, while present, did not try the case. This duty fell to attorneys who worked for the railroad and coal companies. In the Doyle trial the prosecution was headed by General Charles Albright who worked for the Lehigh and Wilkes-Barre Coal Company. The general wore his civil war uniform, including his sword, throughout the trial. One has to wonder how he would have gotten past security today.

On June 21, 1877, within the walls of the Schuylkill County prison (pictured above) in Pottsville six alleged Molly Maguires were executed by hanging.

The prosecution called more than 100 witnesses that established that Doyle was seen in Lansford on the day of the murder. While no one testified that they had seen Doyle murder Jones, he was described as walking quickly toward the murder site and observed running away with a pistol in hand. The defense did not call a single witness in the case. In their summation the defense conceded that Doyle was in Lansford that day, but he was simply looking for work.

The prosecution case was at its weakest when it came to providing a motive for the murder. Detective McParlan's reports to his superiors laid out a scenario that would have provided a motive. According to the detective, Kerrigan (the head of the Mollies in Tamaqua) had been beaten by the policeman Yost. Another Molly, Hugh McGehan, had been blacklisted by the mine foreman, Jones. Kerrigan initiated contact with James Roarity, the head of the Mollies in Coaldale, in order to exact revenge for these perceived wrong-doings. Kerrigan and Roarity decided that McGehan and a man by the name of James Boyle would murder Yost with the assistance of Kerrigan. Doyle and Kelly, again with Kerrigan's help, would take care of Jones.

The only way the prosecution could introduce this evidence would be to call McParlan as a witness. Because McParlan was still gathering information and the use of his testimony would have exposed his identity as a detective, the prosecution went on without him. It didn't matter. On February 1, 1876, the jury pronounced Doyle guilty and on the 23rd he was sentenced to be hanged.

At later trials, McParlan claimed that it was a common practice among the Mollies to trade jobs. This was done to make it difficult for the townspeople to recognize the out of town assailants.

Something of greater importance to the Molly Maguire story took place during the trial. Jimmy Kerrigan confessed. In fact, he produced a 210 page confession and agreed to testify against his fellow Irishmen in return for immunity. This action earned "Powder Keg" Kerrigan a new nickname, he would henceforth be known as "Squealer" Kerrigan.

Based on McParlan's reports and information supplied by Kerrigan, a unit of the Coal and Iron Police led by Captain Linden made a series of arrests. On February 4th this group set out and arrested James Carroll, James Roarity, Thomas Duffy, Hugh McGehan, James Boyle and Alexander Campbell for the murders of Yost and Jones. Six days later the Coal and Iron Police arrested Thomas Munley as a suspect in the murders of Thomas Sanger and William Uren. Another alleged Molly, Dennis Donnelly, would be arrested later for his part in the murders.

Sanger and Uren were shot and killed on September 1, 1875. On that morning Sanger, who was a mine boss, left for work accompanied by Uren who worked for him. While on the road, the duo was attacked by five heavily armed men who shot and killed them both. Sanger had been targeted for evicting Irishmen. Uren was simply in the wrong place at the wrong time.

Following these murders, a one page handbill titled "Strictly Confidential" began circulating in the coalfields. The paper claimed to present facts to be considered by the Vigilance Committee of the Anthracite Coal Region. The document goes on to list a number of murders that had occurred in the region and named the murderers and their residences. In terms of the Sanger and Uren case the handbill states, "On September 1st, 1875 at about 7 A.M. Thomas Sanger, a mining boss, and William Uren, a miner of Raven Run, were shot and fatally wounded by James O'Donnell, alias "Friday," and Thomas Munley, as the unsuspecting victims were on their way to work. Charles O'Donnell, Charles McAllister, and Mike Doyle were present, and accessories to this murder." The information in the handbill was almost certainly based on reports from Detective McParlan, and it is just as probable that it was distributed by the Pinkerton's.

The handbill began circulating in the fall of 1875, on December 10th of that year it would bear fruit. At about 3 in the morning of the 10th Charles and Ellen McAllister were asleep in their home in Wiggans patch. A small child lay between them and Ellen was pregnant. Ellen's mother was also in the house along with her unmarried sons James "Friday" O'Donnell

Joe Farrell stands in front of Jack Kehoe's grave holding the key supplied by a local resident which allowed us entrance to the aged cemetery. Kehoe has been called the "King of the Mollies" but he was almost surely innocent of the crime that sent him to the gallows.

and Charles O'Donnell. Four borders were also asleep in the house including James McAllister who was the brother of Charles.

Charles McAllister was awakened by a crashing noise: the kitchen door being smashed in. He told his wife to stay in bed and ran to the cellar where he made his way to his neighbor's through a door that connected the residences. His wife did not obey; she got up and opened a door that led to the kitchen and was shot and killed. Now pairs of men began searching every bedroom in the house. They brought James McAllister down the stairs into the yard where he freed himself and ran. Shots were fired, and he was hit in the arm but escaped. James O' Donnell also managed to escape. Charles O'Donnell was not so lucky; he was taken outside, and when he struggled free, he was downed by gunshots. Men gathered around his fallen body and emptied their pistols. The shots were fired so close to the body that they burned the flesh. The next day a note was found on the property that stated "You are the killers of Sanger and Uren." Black Jack Kehoe, the man Gowen considered to be the King of the Mollies, was the brother-in-law of both Charles McAllister and Ellen McAllister.

To this day no one knows who the men were who participated in what became known as the Wiggans Patch massacre. What we do know is that Detective McParlan felt responsible. Upon hearing of the killings, he sent a letter of resignation to the Pinkerton office in New York City. In the letter he states, "Now I wake up this morning to find that I am the murderer of Mrs. McAllister." His resignation was not accepted.

Events moved quickly as a series of Molly Maguire trials commenced. The second trial, that of Edward Kelly, began on March 29th. Again, there were no Irish on the jury and the prosecution team was the same. The jury returned a guilty verdict on April 6th, and six days later Kelly was sentenced to be hanged.

After these first two convictions, the Pottsville Courthouse in Schuylkill County was the scene of the next trial. Leading the prosecution in this case would be Franklin Gowen, President of the Philadelphia and Reading Coal and Iron Company. Gowen was well acquainted with the Pottsville Courthouse. As stated previously, he had served as Schuylkill County's District Attorney. The trial started on May 4 and involved the killing of the Tamaqua police officer Benjamin Yost. James Boyle, James Roarity, Hugh McGehan, Thomas Duffy and James Carroll stood accused of the murder.

This trial marked the first appearance of the detective James McParlan as a witness for the prosecution. The informer, Jimmy Kerrigan, would also testify. Just as the trial was getting underway, news spread that the coal and iron police had arrested ten more Mollies in Schuylkill County. Among the ten was Black Jack Kehoe. Kehoe was a respected man active in

Here is Jack Kehoe's Hibernian House looking much as it did the day he was arrested. It is still in operation and run by Kehoe's great-grandson.

On the Day of the rope four alleged Mollies were hanged together at the same time in the old jail in Jim Thorpe. The gallows were built in the middle of the cell block so the condemned men were able to hear the construction prior to their execution.

community affairs who had written to local newspapers denying the existence of an organization known as the Molly Maguires. He was also active in the leadership of the Hibernians. In addition, he had worked his way out of the mines and had much to lose if his leadership of such a group as the Mollies could be proven.

Detective McParlan was the main witness at this trial, and through his testimony, the prosecution was able to leave the impression that the AOH and the Molly Maguires were one and the same. McParlan detailed secret signs and sayings that members used to identify each other. He stated that the chief purpose of the organization was to protect, and, when necessary, seek revenge for members who felt they had been wronged in some manner. In this way he tied the murders and beatings of the mine owners and bosses to the organization. Jimmy Kerrigan also testified and supported McParlan's account.

The defense did call several witnesses in this case including Mrs. Kerrigan who testified that her husband told her he had murdered Yost. She also condemned him for allowing innocent men to take the blame for his crime. While she was being cross examined, one of the jurors became ill. On May 18th the trial was suspended pending his recovery, however his condition did not improve and on May 25th he died of pneumonia. All the work that had gone into the case was lost. The jury was dismissed, and the prisoners returned to the county jail to await a new trial.

Before the second Yost trial began, Alexander Campbell was brought before the court in Mauch Chunk for the murder of John P. Jones. Campbell, like many of the accused Mollies, was born in Ireland. He arrived in Pennsylvania in 1868 where he opened a saloon in Tamaqua. He later moved to the Lansford area where he operated another saloon, the Columbia house. Campbell was viewed by many to be the leader of the Mollies in Carbon County. What made the Campbell trial important was that all agreed he was not present when Jones was killed. He was charged as an accessory before the fact, accused of being involved in the planning of the murder. The prosecution alleged that Kelly, Doyle and Kerrigan spent the night before the killing at Campbell's tavern. The defense countered with several witnesses who said they had been at Campbell's that night and had not seen the three men. After an eleven day trial the jury quickly returned with a guilty verdict and on August 28th Campbell was sentenced to be hanged. Clearly, an Irishman owning a public tavern was a dangerous business to be involved in at the time.

Before Campbell's trial was over, another had begun in Pottsville where Thomas Munley was tried for the murders of Thomas Sanger and William Uren. The prosecution case rested entirely on the testimony of McParlan. Several of Munley's family members testified that he was at home on the day of the murder. Despite this testimony, Munley was found guilty and sentenced to death.

By then, the second Yost trial was underway with the accused being Boyle, Carroll, McGehen and Roarity. Thomas Duffy had requested and was granted a separate trial. McParlan and Kerrigan repeated their testimony and all four men were found guilty. They too were sentenced to be hanged. In addition, the separate trial did not help Duffy as he was also found guilty and received the same sentence.

The Pinkertons continued to investigate past murders including that of mine boss Morgan Powell who had been killed in 1871. Three men, John Donahue, Thomas Fisher and Alec Campbell, were arrested and tried for this murder. All three were convicted and sentenced to death. This was Campbell's second conviction.

The first ten executions took place on June 21, 1877, Black Thursday, or the Day of the Rope as it was referred to by locals. Four of the convicted Irishmen would be hanged in the Mauch Chunk jail. The other six would face the hangman in Pottsville.

The Mauch Chunk hangings occurred first. The gallows had been constructed so that all four men could be hanged at the same time. At around 10:30 in the morning, Alexander Campbell took his place on the gallows. In his final statement, he forgave his executioners. Michael Doyle was next, and he took his spot on the gallows. He said that he had come to this point because of his failure to follow the advice of his church on secret societies. John Donahue took his place and declined comment. Edward Kelly was the last to take his place and, led by his priest, forgave everyone and added that if he had listened to his priests, he would not have found himself on the gallows. The men were then readied for execution and at approximately 10:45, the trap was sprung and the four hurtled to their death. After the bodies were cut down and their hoods removed, the sheriff invited the spectators present to inspect the bodies.

In Pottsville, the authorities had decided to hang the prisoners two at a time. Between 8 and 10 AM, those with official passes were allowed into the prison where they scurried to find the best spots to watch the executions. Meanwhile, the area around the prison, including the hills, were packed with people.

Around 11 AM, the first two prisoners, James Boyle and Hugh McGehan emerged from the jail and made their way to the gallows. Both asked for forgiveness, and Boyle pardoned those who were about to hang him. Ten minutes later, the two were dead. The pair to follow were James Carroll and James Roarity. The latter had been convicted primarily based on the testimony of Jimmy Kerrigan who claimed that Roarity had paid him to have Yost killed. On the gallows, Roarity insisted that this was not so, and he added that Thomas Duffy had nothing to do with the Yost murder. Carroll simply stated that he was an innocent man. Both men were hung at around 12:20. Thomas Duffy and Thomas Munley were the last to the gallows. Neither said much beyond that it was no use and at 1:20, both were sent falling to their death.

At this point the Mollies, if they ever existed, were finished as a power in the coal region. Ten more would be hanged, and others would serve long prison terms. This was not enough to satisfy Franklin Gowen. He wouldn't be happy until he saw Jack Kehoe, who was already serving a seven year prison term, at the end of a rope.

Kehoe was a man who worked his way out of the mines. By 1873, he opened a tavern and rooming house in Girardville called the Hibernian House. He ran this business for three years and during this time became active in local politics. He was elected to the post of Constable in Girardville and was also named Schuylkill County delegate in the AOH. When local newspapers, based on information supplied by the Pinkertons, began linking the Hibernians to the Molly Maguires Kehoe publicly denied such charges. It was Kehoe's view that the Mollies were the fictional invention of the mine owners. Based on information supplied by Detective McParlan,

Kehoe was arrested in 1876 and charged with conspiracy to commit murder. This charge did not carry a death sentence, but Gowen resurrected a murder that occurred in 1862 and named Kehoe one of the killers.

Frank Langdon was a mining boss in Audenried where Kehoe lived and worked. On June 14, 1862, he was assaulted by at least three men. He was able to return home, but he died three days later as a result of the beating. In January of 1877, Kehoe was tried for his murder. The evidence presented at the trial was murky at best. Kehoe was said to have threatened Langdon weeks before he was beaten, but other witnesses claimed to have seen Kehoe on a hotel porch at the time Langdon was assaulted. In his summation, Gowen described Kehoe as a man who made money by his traffic in the souls of his fellow men. Despite the lack of evidence, Kehoe was found guilty and sentenced to death.

Kehoe's lawyers fought the conviction to the State Supreme Court which denied the appeal. Next they petitioned the Board of Pardons where they produced sworn statements from John Campbell and Neil Dougherty (both of whom had been convicted of second degree murder in the matter) admitting their participation in the beating and swearing that Kehoe was not present. In September 1878, the Board voted 2-2 on the petition. A tie vote meant the conviction was upheld.

On December 18, 1878, Kehoe waited in his cell with one of his lawyers, Martin L'Velle. He told L'Velle that he was prepared to die. Shortly thereafter, Kehoe took his place on the gallows in Pottsville. Given the opportunity to speak, he proclaimed his innocence, adding that he had not even seen the crime being committed. After making his statement, Kehoe nodded to the sheriff signifying that he was ready. He was quickly shackled and strapped, and at 10:27 a.m., the trap door was sprung. Four other men would be hanged as Mollies after Kehoe, but public interest in the story and in the hangings was never the same. In September of 1978, the Governor of Pennsylvania, Milton Shapp, released a statement that included the following; "It was Jack Kehoe's popularity among the workingmen that led Franklin Gowen to fear, despise, and ultimately destroy him." On January 12, 1979, Shapp signed a posthumous pardon for Jack Kehoe. This is the only posthumous pardon issued in the history of Pennsylvania.

Kehoe is buried in the old Saint Jerome's Catholic Cemetery in Tamaqua. The two victims of the Wiggans Patch massacre, Ellen McAllister and her brother, Charles O'Donnell, were also laid to rest here. The cemetery is located on the corner of High and Nescopeck streets, and it is fenced in and locked. A neighbor who lives on that corner has a key that he is happy to share with visitors. When we were looking for a way in, he appeared and asked "You here to see Kehoe?" That's how we found our way into the cemetery. Two other alleged Mollies, Thomas Duffy and Jack

Donahue, are also buried there in unmarked graves. Another place worth visiting in relation to Kehoe is his Hibernian House in Girardville, which is now run by his great grandson. Among the artifacts that can be viewed at this location is Kehoe's cell door from the Pottsville prison.

Alec Campbell is buried in Saint Joseph's Catholic cemetery on Ludlow Street in Summit Hill. There are no grave markers in this cemetery due to acts of vandalism. A mock trial of Campbell was held in Jim Thorpe recently using the transcripts from his trial. A relative portrayed Campbell, and he was found innocent. Another alleged Molly, Thomas Fisher, lies there as well.

The Schuylkill County jail in Pottsville where many of the hangings took place is still in operation, but aside from plaques noting what happened, there is little to see. There is one interesting plaque that is on the wall at the jail's main entrance. The plaque notes that the largest mass execution in Pennsylvania history took place inside this prison. It also references the four executions that took place in Mauch Chunk that same day. What is striking is it ends by stating that the pardon of Jack Kehoe reflects "the judgment of many historians that the trials and executions were part of a repression directed against the fledgling mine workers union of that historic period."

Final resting place of Franklin Gowen who was the man most responsible for the hangings of 20 alleged Molly Maguires during the 1870's.

The Carbon County jail, however, is now a museum where regular tours are conducted. A replica of the gallows stands where the original one once stood. In addition, visitors can view the mysterious handprint in cell 17. According to legend, as one of the Mollies (either Alec Campbell or Thomas Fisher) was about to be taken to the gallows, he put his handprint on the wall of his cell saying that it would remain forever as a sign of his innocence. Despite efforts to remove the print, it remains to this day.

Things went well for one of the other main characters in the Molly story. James McParlan was named manager of the Pinkertons' office in Denver Colorado. He passed away in Denver in 1919.

Franklin Gowen eventually lost his leadership position in the Philadelphia and Reading Coal and Iron Company. He returned to private practice. On December 13, 1889, according to the coroner who investigated the death, Gowen shot himself while staying in a hotel in Washington D.C. Many of Gowen's family and friends believed he was murdered. In 2002, a book written by Patrick Campbell (a descendant of Alec Campbell) entitled "Who Killed Franklin Gowen", concludes that Gowen was a homicide victim. Gowen is buried in the Ivy Hill Cemetery just outside Philadelphia.

In 1969, a highly fictionalized major motion picture called "The Molly Maguires" was released. It was filmed largely in Pennsylvania including several scenes that take place in Jim Thorpe. Much of the movie was filmed in Eckley, not far from Hazleton. Eckley in now a museum and visitors are most welcome. In the movie, Richard Harris plays Detective McParlan and Sean Connery stars as Black Jack Kehoe. It's worth a look.

If You Go:

In the center of downtown Jim Thorpe, you can always visit the Molly Maguire Pub where one can find good food and drink at reasonable prices. The pub has a large outdoor deck that is open weather permitting. That same section of Jim Thorpe is home to many antique and specialty shops that you might want to check out.

In addition, the town is quite close to the Pocono's, so white water rafting is available as well as skiing depending on the season. Finally, you can visit the Jim Thorpe Memorial which is the final resting place for that great athlete (see Chapter 26).

22.
"Pennsylvania's Forester"

Gifford Pinchot
County: Pike
Town: Milford
Cemetery: Milford Cemetery
Address: Route 209 - Milford

If you have ever been inconvenienced by Pennsylvania's Liquor Laws, or outraged by the cost of alcoholic beverages in the Commonwealth, you can blame, as we will explain later, Gifford Pinchot. The man had an impressive resume. Among the positions to which he was appointed was the First Chief of the United States Forest Service. In addition, he was elected Governor of Pennsylvania twice, first in 1923 and again in 1931.

Pinchot was born on August 11, 1865 in Connecticut. He was educated at Exeter Academy and Yale. His family had made their fortune in the lumbering business. While not opposed to the wealth this had brought him, Pinchot's father grew to regret the damage that had been done to the land. Reportedly, this guilt resulted in him encouraging Gifford to become a forester. His father's influence proved effective, and Pinchot went to France to study forestry. Upon his return to the United States, he found work as a forest surveyor. Pinchot, by this time, had come to believe in the selective harvesting of forest resources. It was his view that forests could produce timber and yet be maintained for the enjoyment of future generations.

In, 1898, Pinchot was named head of the United States Division of Forestry. In 1900, he founded the Society of American Foresters. The establishment of this organization immediately made the forestry profession more credible. In 1905, President Theodore Roosevelt appointed Pinchot to the post of Chief Forester of the United States Forest Service.

Pinchot rose to national prominence under Roosevelt and he remained at his post when William Taft succeeded Roosevelt in 1909. The Taft administration did not view conservation as a priority, and Pinchot found himself in conflict with Richard Ballinger, the Secretary of the Interior. Taft backed his cabinet member and fired Pinchot. The firing actually pleased Pinchot as he used it to focus public scrutiny on conservation and forest issues.

In 1910, Pinchot founded and funded the National Conservation Association. He would serve as its president for the next 15 years. The

Gifford Pinchot

purpose of the organization was to be a watchdog over the use of public lands and to oppose the transfer of public lands back to the states.

In 1912, Pinchot supported the unsuccessful efforts of Teddy Roosevelt and the Progressive Party. Two years later, he ran for Senate under the Progressive Party banner for a United States Senate seat but he was defeated. He put his political ambitions on hold until 1922 when he ran, as a republican, for Governor of Pennsylvania. His main issues were the economy, the enforcement of prohibition, and the regulation of public utilities. He won by a wide margin. His major push, in his first term as governor, was to create a giant power scheme that would result in the transmission of electricity from plants located near the Pennsylvania coal mines. His critics called it socialism but it did appear years later in the form of the Tennessee Valley Authority.

At the end of his first term, he made another unsuccessful attempt at claiming a United States Senate seat. Failing here, he ran for Governor again in 1930 and won. His second term was marked by his efforts to pave rural roads. He also had to deal with the repeal of prohibition in 1933. He quickly called for a special session of the state legislature that resulted in the State Liquor Control Board and the state-run liquor stores. Pinchot's stated intention was "to discourage the purchase of alcoholic beverages by making it as inconvenient and expensive as possible." A majority of Pennsylvanians would say he succeeded.

Pinchot ran a third time for the United States Senate and was unsuccessful. In 1938, he made another try for the Governor's office but he was defeated. While he never ran for public office again, he did advise President Franklin D. Roosevelt. In his later years he also wrote a book on his life as a forester, and he invented a fishing kit meant for use in lifeboats during World War II.

Pinchot died from Leukemia on October 14, 1946. He was 81. Several sites are named in his honor including, Gifford Pinchot National Forest in Washington, Gifford Pinchot State Park in Pennsylvania, and Pinchot Hall at Penn State University. The house where he was born, Grey Towers, outside of Milford, is now a national historic site. It is open to the public for tours. It also serves as a conservation education and leadership center. Gifford Pinchot is buried in a large mausoleum in the Milford Cemetery.

If You Go:

Just across the narrow road from the Pinchot gravesite, one can find the grave of Charles Henry Van Wyck. He was a Congressman from New York, a Senator from Nebraska and a Brigadier General in the Civil War.

On February 22, 1861, Van Wyck survived an assassination attempt in Washington. This occurred on the same night an alleged attempt was made on President-Elect Abraham Lincoln in Baltimore. The attack on Van Wyck was apparently motivated by a harsh anti-slavery speech he delivered on the floor of the house. In the speech he denounced the southern states for the "crime against the laws of God and nature." He fought off the attack surviving only because a book and papers he carried in his breat pocket blocked the thrust of a Bowie knife.

Also buried in the Milford Cemetery is General Daniel Brodhead. He fought with George Washington on Long Island and wintered with the Continental Army at Valley Forge in 1777-1778.

Here is the final resting place of Pennsylvania's great conservationist and the architect of the Commonwealth's liquor system.

23.
"The Voices of Pittsburgh"

Bob Prince and Myron Cope

Bob Prince
County: Allegheny
Town: Pittsburgh
Cemetery: Westminster Presbyterian Church
Address: 2040 Washington Road

Myron Cope
County: Allegheny
Town: Carnegie
Cemetery: Chartiers Cemetery
Address: 801 Noblestown Road

Bob Prince, known as "the Gunner", was an announcer who was the voice of the Pittsburgh Pirates for 28 years, from 1948 until 1975 and became a Pittsburgh institution. Yet he missed the greatest moment in Pirate history and one of the greatest moments in all of baseball history. The moment took place when Bill Mazeroski hit his World Series winning home run in the bottom of the ninth inning in the 1960 World Series against the New York Yankees that gave the Pirates their first championship in 35 years. He was making his way back from the Pirate Clubhouse where he had been sent to do postgame interviews when it appeared the Pirates would win 9-7. When the Yankees tied it up in the top of the ninth, he was ordered back to the booth. He was in the elevator when the historic and dramatic home run was hit and was told to return to the Pirate clubhouse just as he stepped off the elevator. He was broadcasting the World Series nationwide on NBC and the NBC production people were telling Prince what to do, but not telling him what happened. He had no idea when an NBC staffer directed Mazeroski toward Prince in the exuberant Pirate clubhouse. Prince merely asked Mazeroski how it felt to be a world champion and Mazeroski said "great". Then Prince moved on.

Robert Ferris Prince was born in Los Angelas on July 1 1916. His father, a former West Point football standout, was a career military man and thus young Prince, an army brat, went to many different schools before graduating from Schenley High School in Pittsburgh. He started college at

A terrible towel rests on the tombstone of its inventor, the great Pittsburgh Steeler announcer, Myron Cope.

Here lay the remains of the "Gunner" Bob Prince voice of the Pittsburgh Pirates who announced the first World Series game telecast coast to coast in 1960.

the University of Pittsburgh where he lettered on the swimming team. When his father was transferred and the family moved to California, he transferred to Stanford. He hated Stanford and claimed he flunked out on purpose. Later, after another family move, he enrolled and graduated from the University of Oklahoma with a degree in Business Administration. He then went to Harvard Law School but quit after he landed a job in 1941 as host of "Case of Sports" on WJAS radio in Pittsburgh.

Prince sold insurance during the day and hosted his show in the evening. He made a name for himself among sports fans with his loud, opinionated rants. Once, Prince accused hometown boxer Billy Conn of ducking tough opponents. Conn ran into Prince several nights later at the Pittsburgh Arena and slammed Prince against a wall and threatened to beat him senseless. Ironically, the two later became close friends.

In 1948, Prince was hired by the Pirates to work as the sidekick to beloved Pirate play-by-play man Rosey Roswell. He got along well with Roswell and was promoted to the top spot when Roswell died in February 1955. He became known as "The Gunner" because of his rat-a-tat-tat delivery. He had many descriptive phrases that became known as "Gunnerisms". Some of the most famous are "you can kiss it goodbye!" for a home run, "a bloop and a blast" which he would call when the Pirates were down a run or "by a gnat's eyelash" when describing a close play.

Prince enjoyed an unusual relationship with Pirate players and for many became a friend, confidant, and mentor. He also had a close relationship with former Pirate great and hall of fame outfielder, Ralph Kiner, that included outside business partnerships, and the two drove matching silver Jaguars around Pittsburgh. Prince, who spoke Spanish, became very close to Roberto Clemente, who in 1971, in a public ceremony in Puerto Rico, gave Prince the silver bat he had received in 1961 for winning the National League Batting title.

Prince believed that part of a broadcaster's job was to pull for the home team. He was an unabashed Pirate fan and after every Pirate win, regardless of how the game went, he would yell "We had 'em all the way!". In 1966, he popularized a good luck charm known as the "Green Weenie", a plastic rattle in the shape of an oversized pickle that Pirate fans used to jinx opponents. The idea was derived from pins distributed by the H.J. Heinz factory in Pittsburgh shaped like a pickle. In 1974, Prince invented a similar good luck charm encouraging female fans to wave their "babushkas" to spark a rally.

When he chose to stay focused, Prince could deliver a very accurate, exciting description of the game, but he usually rambled a lot and told stories about anything that popped into his mind. While most Pirate fans seemed to like this, some hated it. He also lived a wild lifestyle, drank a lot, wore colorful flashy clothes, and once in a hotel in St. Louis, leaped from a third floor window into the hotel pool to win a twenty dollar bet. Beneath all the bluster and flamboyance, Prince was a sensitive, caring, and generous man. He co-founded the Allegheny Valley School for Exceptional Children in 1960 to care for children with intellectual and developmental disabilities. Over the years, he raised four million dollars for the school and volunteered countless hours with students at the school.

Despite his popularity, Prince began to clash with his bosses after KDKA purchased the rights to the Pirate broadcasts in 1969. In 1975, Prince and his sidekick Nellie King were fired. Pirate fans and sponsors went berserk. Hundreds of supporters held a rally downtown to show support and several Pirate players including Willie Stargell and Al Oliver spoke to a crowd estimated at 10,000. Their efforts failed and KDKA hired Milo Hamilton to succeed Prince.

The official green weenie created by Bob Prince for use during Pirate games.

A broken hearted Prince had stints with the Houston Astros, Pittsburgh Penguins hockey team, and even on ABC's "Monday Night Baseball" but he wasn't himself and each ended after a short time. He drifted from job to job, many of which were considered small for a celebrity of his stature. Eventually, he returned to baseball when in 1982 a cable station hired him to do Pirate games. Exposure was limited since cable did not have many subscribers and they offered only a small selection of games.

In 1985, Prince, a smoker, was diagnosed with mouth cancer. Shortly after surgery to remove a tumor between his tongue and jaw, he was hired by the Pirates to return to fulltime duty as a member of the regular radio broadcast team. On May 3, 1985, Bob Prince returned to the Pirate radio booth. The crowd gave him a standing ovation and the Pirates scored nine runs in his first inning of broadcasting. Prince's return to the booth lasted just two more games. He became ill on May 20 while sitting through a rain delay and returned to the hospital. He died 21 days later on June 10, 1985 at the age of 68. Prince was posthumously awarded the Ford Frick Award by the Baseball Hall of Fame in 1986.

Bob Prince's remains are at the Westminster Presbyterian Church in Upper Saint Clair, just south of Pittsburgh. A book on Prince titled "We Had 'Em All the Way" by Jim O'Brien was published in 1998.

The Other famous voice of Pittsburgh is the "voice of the Pittsburgh Steelers," Myron Cope. He was born Myron Sidney Kopelman on January 23, 1929 in Pittsburgh to Jewish parents of Lithuanian descent. A graduate of Taylor Allderdice High School and the University of Pittsburgh in 1951, he was a journalist before becoming a broadcaster. His first job after college was with the Erie Times, but he was soon hired by the Pittsburgh Post-Gazette as a general assignment reporter. It was then that his byline became Myron Cope. During the 1960's, several of his freelance sports articles were published in magazines such as *The Saturday Evening Post* and *Sports Illustrated*. In 1963, Cope received the E.P. Dutton Prize for "Best Magazine Sportswriting in the Nation" for a piece on Cassius Clay. At its 50th anniversary, Sports Illustrated selected Cope's profile of Howard Cosell as one of the fifty best pieces ever published in the magazine. In 1964, Cope published his first book co-written with Jim Brown called "Off My Chest". It was a controversial book in which Jim Brown expressed his opinions about racial injustice in sports.

In 1968, a radio station in Pittsburgh hired Cope to do a brief sports show during the morning commute hours. Cope, who had a nasally voice, a Pittsburgh accent, and an unusual speech pattern did not get positive reviews at first, but gradually listeners realized the quality of his broadcasts and warmed to his style. His popularity grew.

Cope married Mildred Lindberg in 1965, and their son Daniel was born with severe autism. Cope devoted much of his energy to causes addressing autism and spoke candidly about his experiences as a parent of a child with autism and about his efforts to better educate the public about autism. His son lived most of his life at the Allegheny Valley School previously mentioned as having been co-founded by Bob Prince.

In 1970, he was hired as a color analyst for Pittsburgh Steelers radio broadcasts and remained in that role for thirty-five years, the longest term with a single team in NFL history. Over the years he became known for unique catch-phrases and nicknames. He often used Yiddish expressions and became known for his use of "Yoi" or sometimes "Double Yoi" during a broadcast. He is the creator of phrases such as "Steel Curtain" and "Immaculate Reception" and for nicknames such as "The Bus" for Jerome Bettis, "Jack Splat" for Jack Lambert and "Slash" for Kordell Stewart. He also used the term "Cincinnati Bungles" to describe the play of the Bengals

Here lies Edward Rynearson who founded the National Honor Society. For some reason neither of us was extended an invitation to apply for membership. We are as confused as you are.

during the 1990's.

In 1973, Cope began hosting his own radio talk show and in 1975, he invented the Pittsburgh Steelers' Terrible Towel, their famed good luck symbol. It is arguably the best known symbol of any pro sports team. In 1996, Cope gave the rights to the Terrible Towel to the Allegheny School. The proceeds have raised over three million dollars for the school.

In 2002, he published his autobiography, "Myron Cope: Double Yoi!", a touching and humorous memoir. In 2005, he announced his retirement citing health concerns. He had broadcast five Super Bowls and became the first pro football announcer elected to the National Radio Hall of Fame. He died of respiratory failure on February 27, 2008. Two days after his death, hundreds of people gathered in heavy snow in front of City Hall in Pittsburgh to honor Cope. Included in the ceremony was one minute of silent Terrible Towel waving. He is buried in Chartiers Cemetery just south of Pittsburgh. There were Terrible Towels on his grave when we visited.

If You Go:

Chartiers is a nice cemetery with friendly and helpful staff. Buried near Myron Cope are two Congressional Medal of Honor recipients, both from the Civil War. James H. Bronson was born a slave. He enlisted into Company D of the 5th U. S. Colored Infantry Regiment. He was awarded the Medal of Honor for his actions at the Battle of Chaffin's Farm, Virginia in 1864.

James Lemuel Carey is also buried nearby. He was awarded the Medal of Honor for action on April 9, 1865 at Appomattox Courthouse, Virginia. Also buried in Charters Cemetery is Edward Rynearson an educator and founder of the National Honor Society.

John Fulton Reynolds

24.
"A True American Hero"

General John Fulton Reynolds
County: Lancaster
Town: Lancaster
Cemetery: Lancaster Cemetery
Address: 205 East Lemon Street

John Reynolds gave his life for his country during the Battle of Gettysburg. He was one of the Union Army's most respected senior commanders. He fought in the Battles of Second Bull Run, Fredericksburg, Chancellorsville, and Gettysburg. He was captured in June 1862 and held prisoner at the infamous Libby Prison in Richmond. Within two months Reynolds was exchanged for Lloyd Tilghman, a Confederate general who was killed at the Battle of Champion Hill. President Lincoln offered Reynolds command of the entire Army of the Potomac but he turned it down because he thought he would not be given a free hand. It was Reynolds opinion that previous commanders had become bogged down due to political influences.

John Reynolds was born in Lancaster, Pennsylvania on September 20, 1820. He was one of nine children. Two of his brothers would also go on to have distinguished military careers. He was educated in local schools. The future President, Senator James Buchanan, nominated Reynolds to attend the United States Military Academy in 1837. He graduated in 1841, 26th in a class of 50.

Reynolds experienced his first real military action during the Mexican War. During the war, he served under General Zachary Taylor and performed quite well. He received two promotions during the conflict. Reynolds was made a captain as a result of his gallantry during the Battle of Monterrey. During the Battle of Buena Vista, his unit prevented the Mexican Army from outflanking the Americans. This earned him the rank of major. During this conflict, he befriended both Winfield Scott Hancock and Lewis A. Armistead. Hancock would be a fellow Union officer at Gettysburg, where he would be wounded. Armistead, would fight on the Confederate side, and be killed on the third day of the battle at the high point of the Confederate advance during Picket's charge.

After the Mexican War, Reynolds remained in the Army. He was stationed in Oregon and he took part in the 1857 Utah War with the

MAJOR GEN.
JOHN F. REYNOLDS
COMMANDING
LEFT WING 1st 3rd & 11th CORPS
ARMY OF THE POTOMAC
JULY 1st 1863
ERECTED BY THE
STATE OF PENNSYLVANIA
JULY 1886

This monument marks the spot where Reynolds fell on the initial day of the Battle of Gettysburg.

Mormons. Returning east, he became the Commandant of Cadets at West point from 1860-1861. Here he trained men some of whom fought on the Union side, and some who rallied to the Confederacy during the Civil War.

Shortly after the War between the States began, Reynolds was promoted to the rank of brigadier general. Major General George McClellan took steps to see to it that Reynolds was assigned to the just created Army of the Potomac. He was put in charge of a brigade of Pennsylvania volunteers.

The first major battle he fought in was the Battle of Beaver Creek Dam. The confederates launched a major attack on June 26,1862, but Reynolds held his position. The confederates attacked again the next day. Reynolds had gone 48 hours without sleep. Believing he was safe, he found a place to get some rest. The Union's retreating troops left him behind, and he was captured. The confederates who took him prisoner brought him before their General D. H. Hill. Hill and Reynolds were friends from before the war and Hill told Reynolds not to feel badly, that this is what happened in wars. As detailed earlier, the Union quickly arranged a prisoner exchange that resulted in Reynolds release.

Reynolds, upon his release, quickly distinguished himself on the field of battle. On the second day of the Second Battle of Bull Run, the Union Army was disorganized and in a mass retreat. Reynolds led his men in a risky counterattack. It proved a success, giving the Union Army time to regroup and retreat in an orderly fashion. There are those that believe that without Reynolds the Union troops may have been totally defeated that day.

The Battle of Chancellorsille took place in May of 1863, and resulted in a major Union defeat. Reynolds was highly upset with the Commander of the Army at the time, Major General Hooker. After being overun by a Stonewall Jackson flank attack, Hooker called his generals together. Three of the five generals urged Hooker to stay on the offensive, but he decided to retreat. Reynolds said in a manner that he intended Hooker to hear, "What was the use of calling us together at this time of night when he intended to retreat anyhow?"

Reynolds final appearance on the field of battle was at Gettysburg. Brigadier General John Buford, a Union Cavalry officer, arrived in the small Pennsylvania town first. He occupied the town and set up defensive lines outside of town on high ground that he believed ideal to repel attacks. When General Buford decided to try to hold the high ground on Day 1 of the Battle of Gettysburg, he did so partly because it was John Reynolds who was supposed to arrive with his infantry. He respected Reynolds and believed he would arrive in time to relieve his cavalry troops. Buford did hold the ground for Reynolds, who arrived as fighting was underway. After a conference with Buford, Reynolds led his soldiers to the front lines and was

THE FALL OF REYNOLDS.

putting them in place when he was downed by a shot, from what most believe was a confederate sniper. He died instantly and his command was assumed by Major General Abner Doubleday who would become famous for creating America's national pastime.

Reynolds was the first and highest ranking General to die at Gettysburg. He was loved by his men, and historian Shelby Foote wrote that many considered him the best general in the army. His body was transported to Lancaster where he was buried on July 4, 1863. He was only 42.

Reynolds was so important to the Union effort and so highly thought of that he is memorialized by three statues in Gettysburg National Park (McPherson Ridge, The National Cemetery, and the Pennsylvania Memorial). There is also a statue of Reynolds in front of the Philadelphia City Hall.

The spot on the Gettysburg battlefield where Reynolds fell is marked by a momument. His grave is in Lancaster Cemetery near the entrance and one of the best kept in the old cemetery.

If You Go:

There are a number of other Civil War veteran's graves in Lancaster Cemetery including John Reynolds' older brother, Rear Admiral William Reynolds, who served as commander on the USS New Hampshire in the Union Navy's blockade of the Southern Ports. Two Brevet Brigadier

Monument honoring John Reynolds on the Gettysburg battlefield.

Generals, Henry Hambright and Samuel Ross, are also buried there as well as Colonel David Miles, who was captured at the Battle of Chickamauga and confined to Libby Prison. He successfully escaped, and returned to Union army where he led a brigade in Sherman's March to the Sea. In addition, President James Buchanan, who was instrumental in getting Reynolds accepted to West Point, is buried in Lancaster. The former President (See Chapter 2) is buried in Woodland Hill Cemetery. Visitors to Lancaster may also want to check out Chapter 20 on Thomas Mifflin.

Base of monument marking the grave of General John Reynolds in Lancaster.

25.
"The Cop That Would Be King"

Frank Rizzo
County: Philadelphia
Town: Philadelphia
Cemetery: Holy Sepulchre Cemetery
Address: 3301 Cheltenham Ave

Francis "Frank" Lazarro Rizzo was an American police officer and politician. He served two terms as mayor of Philadelphia from January 1972 to January 1980. He served as Police Commissioner for four years prior to becoming mayor. Mr. Rizzo was one of those seemingly larger than life figures, destined to be a hero to some and a villain to others.

He was born October 23, 1920 in Philadelphia to a police family. After a brief stint in the US Navy and three years working in a steel mill, he became a policeman in 1943, rising through the ranks to become Police Commissioner in 1967. He served in that role during the turbulent years of 1967-1971. Known as a cop's cop, he showed his mettle when, with a nightstick protruding from the cummerbund of his tuxedo, he left a black tie affair in order to lead "my men" to break up a riot. While serving as Commissioner, he expanded the police force, won the loyalty of his men, and kept the crime rate below that of any other major city. He was, however, accused of racism and police brutality. Supporters noted that in his five year tenure, Philadelphia had the lowest crime rate of the nation's ten largest cities. His detractors said the price for that order was intolerable. In 1970, shortly before he resigned to run for mayor, the police deeply embittered Philadelphia blacks by raiding the Black Panther headquarters, herding them into the street, and ordering them to strip naked in front of TV cameras and reporters. "Imagine the big Black Panthers with their pants down," Mr. Rizzo gloated at the time.

In 1971, Rizzo ran for mayor using "Firm but Fair" as his slogan and won as a law and order Democrat. As Mayor Rizzo continued to support the strong-arm tactics of the police department, he himself made use of them, forming a secret police force that investigated his political opponents. His rough edges and penchant for bombastic statements frequently inflamed his enemies. Two of his most famous quotes are: "Just wait until after November, I'm gonna make Attila the Hun look like a faggot" and "a liberal is a conservative who hasn't been mugged yet".

Statue of Frank Rizzo

Rizzo had a controversial relationship with the media including Andrea Mitchell, who was one of the first female urban beat reporters. Almost immediately after he had been elected Mayor, *The Philadelphia Inquirer* began running a series of articles detailing Rizzo's years as police commissioner. The articles did not compliment the new mayor. In addition, Richard Dilworth, a former Philadelphia mayor, went public with allegations that Rizzo had used the police force for his own political purposes. Rizzo, by this time, had few supporters in the press, as he had hired about two dozen reporters who had written about him while he was commissioner in a positive manner. What Rizzo accomplished was the removal of his biggest supporters from the media.

Rizzo's problems with the press did not ease as he went further into his first term. In one incident, Rizzo was accused by the Democratic Party Chairman, Peter Camiel, of offering jobs in exchange for choosing certain candidates for other city offices. Rizzo responded by calling Camiel a liar. A reporter from the Philadelphia Daily News asked Rizzo if he would take a polygraph test to prove Camiel was lying. Both men agreed to take the test. "If this machine says a man lied, he lied," Rizzo said before taking the test. The test results showed that Rizzo appeared to be lying and Camiel appeared to be truthful. The scandal was widely reported and severely damaged his reputation and chances of becoming Governor. At this point, Rizzo severed his relationship with the media and didn't hold a press conference for almost two years.

Campaigning for a second term in 1975, Rizzo's slogan was, "He held the line on taxes." Almost immediately after his victory in the election, he convinced city council to raise the taxes. The move angered fiscal conservatives who had supported Rizzo during the campaign. Another development during his second term was the taking over by the city of the Philadelphia Gas Works. Formerly considered one of the best managed municipal utilities in the country, it soon became a long-running fiscal and management embarrassment to the city due to generous municipal labor contracts and the expansion of patronage hiring. Rizzo himself would serve as a security consultant at the Gas Works from 1983-1991.

Rizzo's actions during his second term resulted in a well organized effort for a recall election. As a matter of fact, the organizers of the effort collected well over the 250,000 signatures required to force the recall. Rizzo supporters responded by challenging the validity of the signatures and the constitutionality of the recall procedure. Polls showed that Rizzo would lose a recall election by a wide margin, but he managed to survive when the Pennsylvania Supreme Court, by a single vote, declared the recall process unconstitutional. The Supreme Court decision was written by Chief Justice Robert Nix. Nix had been elected to the court in 1971 with Rizzo's support.

As mayor, Rizzo continued to champion the idea that strong and severe law enforcement methods were necessary in light of rising crime rates. By 1979, the issue had been moved into the courtroom. The Justice Department filed suit in the United States District Court, charging Mayor Rizzo and other high ranking city officials with committing or condoning "widespread and severe" acts of police brutality. A federal judge later dismissed the suit saying the government had no grounds to have filed it in the first place.

Rizzo wanted a third consecutive term in 1979 but was facing a two term consecutive term limit in the City Charter. He got the City Council to place a question on the ballot that would have allowed him to run. In a record turnout, Philadelphians voted two to one against the change, thus blocking him from running in 1979. He ran again for Mayor in 1983 but lost the Democratic nomination to Wilson Goode. In 1985, he switched to the Republican Party and ran again in 1987, but lost the general election again to Wilson Goode. He was running for Mayor again in 1991 when on July 16, Frank Rizzo died of a massive heart attack. Frank Rizzo's funeral was large and carried on live television. He is buried with family members in Holy Sepulchre Cemetery in Cheltenham.

A statue of mayor Rizzo waving one of his arms in greeting, stands in front of Philadelphia's Municipal Services Building. A book by Joseph

Hizzoner Frank Rizzo.

Daughen and Peter Binzen titled "The Cop Who Would Be King" is considered an authoritative account of Rizzo's rise to power.

If You Go:

See the Chapter 16 on Connie Mack. Also buried at Holy Sepulchre Cemetery are three other noteworthy Pennsylvanians:

John B. Kelly Sr., also known as Jack Kelly, was one of the greatest American oarsmen in the history of the sport. He was a triple Olympic Gold Medal winner and once won 126 straight races in a single scull, including six U.S. National Championships. He was also the father of Grace Kelly, the actress who became Princess of Monaco.

Robert N.C. Nix, Jr., was the first African American Chief Justice of any state's highest court and the first to be elected to statewide office in Pennsylvania. He served as a justice of the Supreme Court of Pennsylvania for 24 years, 12 of which were as Chief Justice.

Michael McKeever was awarded the Congressional Medal of Honor for his bravery at Burnt Ordinary Virginia (now Toano, Virginia) on January 19, 1836. His citation reads "was one of a small scouting party that charged and routed a mounted force of the enemy six times their number. He led the charge in a most gallant manner, going beyond the call of duty."

Jim Thorpe

26.
"The Greatest Athlete of the 20th Century"

Jim Thorpe
County: Carbon
Town: Jim Thorpe
Cemetery: Jim Thorpe Memorial
Address: 101 East 10th Street

The man who many consider to be the greatest athlete of his time is buried in Pennsylvania in the town that bears his name. Jim Thorpe excelled at multiple sports, though he is best remembered for his accomplishments in football and in track and field. It was as a direct result of his play in these two areas that from 1996-2001 he was awarded ABC's Wide World of Sports Athlete of the Century award.

Thorpe was born on May 22, 1888 in Oklahoma on a Sac-and-Fox Indian reservation. Thorpe's youth, not unlike his adult life, was filled with ups and downs. His father recognized his athletic ability and encouraged young Thorpe to develop it. Among his favorite childhood games was chasing (on foot) and catching wild horses. He was also a big fan of follow the leader, though when he was the leader you would have to do things like climb trees and jump to the ground as well as swim across rivers. Thorpe was also known to run the 20 miles home from school each day. He thrived at competing with others.

As mentioned above, there were also childhood disappointments. Few in his family were blessed with long lives. His twin brother passed away when he was 8. Both of his parents died when he was in his teens. He took his father's death extremely hard.

When Thorpe was 16 he was recruited to attend the Carlisle Indian School in Carlisle, Pennsylvania. It was here that his athletic ability caught the attention of the legendary coach Glen "Pop" Warner. One day Thorpe was walking past the field where the track team was practicing. He stopped to watch and noticed how no one could clear the high bar that was set at 5 feet 9 inches. Despite the fact that he was in his street clothes, he walked onto the field and cleared the height easily.

Thorpe enjoyed great success in track and field while attending Carlisle. For example, in 1909 he almost beat the Lafayette team by himself when he won six events. The Lafayette coach, Harold Anson Bruce, said he

Jim Thorpe as a member of the New York Giants.

had never seen such a natural athlete. But it was on the football field where Thorpe really made a name for himself. Pop Warner was initially against Thorpe playing football because he felt his star track and field athlete might get hurt. Finally, Thorpe convinced him to let him run a few plays in practice. On two successive plays Thorpe galloped for touchdowns untouched. After the exhibition, Thorpe walked over to Warner tossed him the football and said, "Nobody is going to tackle Jim."

By 1911, Pop Warner was calling Thorpe "the greatest all-around athlete in the world." That year, Carlisle was to play the powerful Harvard football team in Cambridge. Thorpe was outstanding at running the ball, using his strength and remarkable speed to consistently advance its position. One reporter noted that he was amazing at avoiding tacklers in the open field. Thorpe was responsible for all of Carlisle's points. While scoring a touchdown and kicking four field goals, he led his team to a 18-15 upset win. Thorpe's play during the season earned him All-American honors.

While 1911 was a great year for Thorpe, it could not compare to his accomplishments in 1912. The 1912 Olympics were held in Stockholm that summer and Thorpe was a member of team USA. First he won the pentathlon a competition that included five different events. Six days later he competed in the decathlon where he set a world record with 8,412 points. What is remarkable about this total is that if Thorpe had posted the

Jim Thorpe at 1912 Olympics

identical marks in the 1948 Olympics he would have won the silver medal. In fact his time of 4 minutes 40.1 seconds in the 1500 meter race would not be beaten until the 1972 Olympics.

After his Olympic performance he was congratulated by King Gustav V of Sweden. The king told Thorpe, "Sir, you are the greatest athlete in the world." Thorpe replied, "Thanks, king."

Thorpe returned to the United States as a national hero. New York City honored him with a ticker tape parade. At the conclusion of the parade Thorpe remarked, "I heard people yelling my name and I couldn't realize how one fellow could have so many friends."

That fall he returned to Carlisle to resume his football career playing for Pop Warner. One of the teams he faced was Army, whose roster included a cadet named Dwight Eisenhower. Carlisle won easily 27-6, and Thorpe put on a spectacular performance. On one play, he galloped 92 yards for a touchdown only to have the play nullified due to a penalty. On the next play he went 97 yards for the score. His play obviously impressed the future president who spoke of Thorpe in a 1961 speech. Ike said, "Here and there, there are some people who are extremely endowed. My memory goes back to Jim Thorpe. He never practiced in his life, and he could do anything better than any other football player I ever saw."

Carlisle went undefeated in 1912 and was widely acknowledged as the national champion. Thorpe won All-American honors again and he found himself sitting on top of the athletic world. There was, however, trouble on the horizon.

A writer for the Worcester Mass. Telegram named Roy Johnson published a story stating that Thorpe had been paid to play semi-pro baseball in 1909 and 1910. During this time, it was not unusual for college athletes to play semi-pro, but most played under different names to avoid losing their amateur status. Thorpe made the mistake of playing under his real name.

As a result of this revelation, the Amateur Athletic Union asked Thorpe for an explanation. Thorpe replied in writing saying, "I hope I will be partly excused by the fact I was simply an Indian schoolboy and did not know about such things. I was not very wise in the ways of the world and did not realize this was wrong." There was not at the time any good reason for not accepting Thorpe's explanation. The Athletic Union thought otherwise and withdrew Thorpe's amateur status retroactively. The International Olympic Commission followed suit by declaring Thorpe a professional athlete. As a result, Thorpe was stripped of his Olympic titles and his gold medals. Almost immediately Thorpe began receiving offers from professional teams.

In 1913 baseball was the most popular sport in the country. It was also, arguably, Thorpe's weakest sport. He signed with the New York Giants where he played in the outfield for three seasons. Thorpe played six seasons of professional baseball, from 1913 to 1915 and from 1917 to 1919. His career totals in baseball are unimpressive. He played in 289 games and had a career batting average of .252. He scored 91 runs and drove in another 82. His career in the big leagues was over though he did continue to play minor league ball until he hung up his bat and glove for good in 1922.

Professional football was in its infancy and nowhere near as popular as it is today. That didn't stop Thorpe from signing with the Canton Bulldogs in 1915. The Bulldogs paid Thorpe $250 per game an amount that in current dollar terms would exceed $5,000. This was considered a very lucrative wage. At the time, Canton's average attendance per game was about 1,200 fans. When Thorpe made his debut, 8,000 paying customers attended the game. Thorpe and the Bulldogs were successful in winning league titles in 1916, 1917, and 1919. With little time left in the 1919 title game, the Bulldogs were forced to punt from deep in their own territory. Thorpe, with the wind at his back, took the snap and kicked a 95 yard punt sealing the victory and the championship.

While playing for the Bulldogs, Thorpe was named the league's President, a post he held for one year. He continued to coach and play for Canton until he joined the Oorang Indians in 1921. He was with this team, made up of all Native Americans, through 1923. While the team did poorly, Thorpe played well enough to be named to the first ALL-NFL team in 1923. Thorpe never won an NFL championship and retired from football in 1928 at the age of 41.

It was recently discovered that Thorpe also had a basketball career. In 1926, he was the star player for the "World Famous Indians" of Larue. His team played exhibitions in New York, Pennsylvania, and Ohio. The fact that he was a basketball player came to light in 2005 when a ticket to one of his games was discovered in an old book.

After Thorpe's athletic career ended, he led a troubled life. His first two marriages, which produced eight children, ended in divorce. One son, Jim Jr. died at the age of two. Thorpe's drinking, which had always been a problem, grew worse. It was not unusual for his drinking binges to end in fights. He also found holding a steady job difficult. He worked many odd jobs that included painting, digging ditches, serving as a deck hand, and a bar bouncer. In the 1930's he appeared in a few short films, usually playing an Indian.

By 1950, Thorpe was broke. That same year, the nation's press named him the most outstanding athlete of the first half of the 20th Century. He did receive about $15,000 from Warner Brothers in 1951 when the movie "Jim Thorpe All-American" was released. The film starred Burt

Here is the final resting place (at least for now) of the man that was called the greatest athlete in the world.

Another section of the Jim Thorpe Memorial that tells the story of his life.

Lancaster in the role of Thorpe and was a big hit.

In 1953, Thorpe was living with his third wife in a trailer in Lomita, California. While eating dinner on March 28th Thorpe suffered his third heart failure. Artificial respiration was used, and it revived him for a short time before he died. He was 64.

Thorpe's athletic achievements have been recognized by many organizations. In 1951, he was elected to the College Football Hall of Fame. In 1963 he was named a Charter Enshrinee in the Pro Football Hall of Fame. He is also a member of the Track and Field Hall of Fame. In 1986, the Jim Thorpe award was created. It is awarded annually to the best defensive back in college football.

After his death, supporters of Thorpe pushed to have his Olympic titles reinstated. Thirty years later their efforts proved successful. On January 18, 1983, commemorative medals were presented to Thorpe's children. He was once again declared an Olympic champion.

In 1954, the towns of Mauch Chunk and East Mauch Chunk merged to form the town now known as Jim Thorpe. Town leaders made a deal with Thorpe's third wife to have his remains moved there in 1954. The town erected the Jim Thorpe Memorial which currently house the great athlete's remains. In June of 2010, Thorpe's son Jack filed a federal lawsuit seeking to have his father's remains retuned to Oklahoma. The case is pending.

If You Go:
See Chapter 21 on the Molly Maguires.

"Big Bill" Tilden

27.
"Big Bill"

Bill Tilden
County: Philadelphia
Town: Philadelphia
Cemetery: Ivy Hill Cemetery
Address: 1201 Easton Road Philadelphia, Pa.

Many have called the 1920's the Golden Age of Sports. Athletic heroes appeared from the beginning of the decade. In baseball, the big names included Babe Ruth, Lou Gehrig, and Ty Cobb. In football, Knute Rockne and his Four Horsemen along with Red Grange commanded the attention of the masses. Bobby Jones and Walter Hagen ruled the golfing world. In men's tennis, one man dominated the game like no one ever had. His name was Bill Tilden.

William (Bill) Tatem Tilden II was born on February 10, 1893 in Philadelphia. His family was wealthy, but they had been stung by the death of three of Bill's older siblings. His mother died when he was 15, and though his father could have easily looked after Tilden, he was sent to live with an aunt who lived in the same neighborhood. When he was 19, he lost his dad and an older brother. He suffered from severe depression for months.

Encouraged by his aunt, he began to concentrate on tennis. Compared to many of his peers, who had been playing for years, 19 was a bit old to begin taking the game seriously. He was not considered good enough to make his college team, which may explain why he dropped out of the University of Pennsylvania to work on his game. That is exactly what he did, not only practicing, but studying the game. By the early twenties, Tilden was ready to make his move.

In 1920, Tilden was 27 years of age and relatively unknown. All that was about to change. Starting in 1920, Tilden led the United States team to seven consecutive Davis Cup Championships. As of today, no other nation has equaled that record. In 1920, Tilden won his first United States National Championship (what would now be considered the United States Open). He would go on to win five more in succession. In 1929, Bill won the tournament again, giving him a total of seven titles. He also participated in the men's doubles event, winning that five times, and mixed doubles where he won four titles. Tilden competed abroad as well. He competed at Wimbledon six times and won in 1920, 1921, and 1930. After his 1930 win, needing money, Tilden turned professional. His career record as an amateur was 71-7 which equates to an incredible winning percentage of .910.

Tilden's professional career began in 1931 when he was 37 years old. The professional tennis tour was in its infancy, having only just begun in 1927. For the next 15 years, Tilden traveled across the United States and Europe competing against other professionals. He was no longer able to win matches whenever he wanted. His opponents included Ellsworth Vines and Don Budge, both of whom had been ranked number one in the world far more recently than Tilden. He was able to hold his own with these young players, but more importantly, he was the number one box office draw on the tour. To give you an idea of how competitive he was, in 1945, he teamed up with Vinnie Richards and won the professional doubles championship. At the time he was 52 years old.

How good was Tilden? Nicknamed "Big Bill" (he stood at six feet one inch), he was a tennis master. He possessed what was described as a cannonball serve. Many who saw him play believed that he often took a little something off his initial service because he disliked short volleys. He was a superb backcourt player, using multiple types of shots to outwit and overpower his opponents. Jack Kramer, who became the number one player in the world in the early 1950's, played against Tilden when he was a teenager and Bill was in his late 40's. Kramer later recalled that Tilden's service was good, and he had a forehand that couldn't be stopped. Kramer said Bill could put the ball anywhere he wanted it.

Tilden was also a student of the game. He even wrote a few books on the subject including, "Match Play and the Spin of the Ball." For years, this book was the tennis player's bible, and it is still in print and available today. Bill was a master of tennis tactics, and he had no equal in recognizing an opponent's strengths and using them to his benefit.

Tilden was also a showman. As a professional, he felt it was his job to sell tickets. Many believed he would deliberately lose the opening set of a match to peak the audience's interest. Sometimes when he was serving to win a match, he would pick up four balls in one hand and quickly fire four aces at his opponent.

Tilden's life off the tennis court was not nearly as successful. He was never known to have a sexual relationship with a woman. As he grew older, he appeared more feminine. Rumors about his homosexuality were both public and well known. In 1946, he was arrested in Indiana for soliciting an underage male prostitute. While in the custody of police, he signed a confession. Some stories claim that he never read the confession because he didn't have his glasses with him. It has been said that he was so vain, he didn't like to wear them. As a result of this arrest, he was sentenced to one year in prison (he served a little over seven months) and five years of probation. In 1949, he was arrested again. In this instance he had picked

A modest tombstone lies over the greatest tennis player of his time.

up a 16 year old hitchhiker who later sued him, claiming the incident had harmed him physically and emotionally. This case concluded with Tilden spending 10 months in jail. He emerged from prison a pariah in the tennis world. Clubs would not give him access to their courts to provide tennis lessons. In addition, he was not invited to play in many tournaments. To aid him in securing an income, his good friend Charlie Chaplin permitted Tilden to use his private court to provide lessons.

In spite of the above incidents, Tilden had his defenders. These people noted that he had never made sexual advances aimed at other players or any of his students. It was their view that Tilden was the victim of the rumors that surrounded him at the time.

Despite his problems, tennis honors continued to come his way. In 1950, the Associated press released a poll citing the greatest athletes of the first half of the 20th century. Among those named in their respective sports were Jim Thorpe, Jack Dempsey, Babe Ruth, and Bobby Jones. Tilden was named the greatest tennis player by a wider margin than any other athlete named in the poll. In 1958, he was inducted into the Tennis Hall of Fame. In addition, when Jack Kramer released his autobiography in 1979, he named Tilden one of the six greatest tennis players of all time.

In 1953, while getting ready to leave for Cleveland where the United States Professional Championship was being held, Tilden suffered a stroke and died. He is buried in a very modest grave in Ivy Hill Cemetery in Philadelphia.

If You Go:

See the "If You Go" section in Chapter 1 on Willie Anderson.

Mary Virginia "Ginnie" or "Jennie" Wade

28.
"A Tragic Love Story"

Ginnie Wade
County: Adams
Town: Gettysburg
Cemetery: Evergreen Cemetery
Address: 799 Baltimore Street

On June 26, 1863, the Confederate troops first entered Gettysburg, and for a twenty year old local girl, it was a scary and frantic day. Her brother Samuel Wade had been arrested by the Confederates for failing to obey orders to hand over the family horse to Confederate troops. Mary Virginia (Ginnie or Jennie) Wade was helping to care for Isaac Brinkerhoff, a six year old disabled neighborhood boy, when she heard of her brother's arrest and went to try to secure an arrest release from General Jubal Early.

Mary Wade was born on Baltimore Street in Gettysburg on May 21, 1843. When she grew older, she worked as a seamstress with her mother in their house on Breckenridge Street while her father was in a mental asylum. When Union troops arrived on July 1 and shooting began, Ginnie went to her sister's house on Baltimore Street in order to provide assistance to her sister Georgia McClellan with her newborn baby. She never expected that the McClellan house would be situated between Union and Confederate lines during the three day battle.

As the fighting wore on, Union troops began asking the family for food and water. Surely Ginnie must have thought of her fiancé Johnston (Jack) Skelly who was serving as a member of the 87th Pennsylvania Volunteer Infantry. She and Skelly and their friend Wesley Culp had been schoolmates who became close friends and often played together on nearby Culp's Hill. Wesley Culp had moved to Virginia and enlisted with the 2nd Virginia Infantry and was now engaged in a great battle on the farm where he was born and raised. Ginnie decided to do what she could for the Union troops and spent her time filling canteens and baking bread. What she didn't know was that her beloved Jack Skelly had been badly wounded and captured by the Confederates at the battle of Carter's Woods near Winchester Virginia. Wesley Culp also fought in that battle against her friend, a brother William, and a cousin David Culp. Wesley Culp actually met up with the wounded Skelly after the battle, and Skelly gave him a message for Ginnie Wade should he make it back to Gettysburg some day.

Culp did manage to slip away from the fighting to visit his two sisters on the Culp farm but discovered Ginnie had left her home to stay at her sister's and was in the crossfire between the lines. Shortly after, on July 2, Wesley Culp was killed within sight of the house where he had been born. He was never able to deliver his message to Ginnie Wade.

Ginnie had worked hard for two days but on July 3, 1863, she awoke at 4:30 in the morning to prepare bread for the union soldiers. Soon after, the house came under confederate fire. Georgia McClellan later noted the last words Ginnie spoke to her. According to Georgia, Ginnie said, "If there is anyone in this house that is to be killed today, I hope it is me." According to Georgia, Ginnie didn't want any harm to come her sister's way because she had a baby.

That day around 8:30 am, Ginnie was kneading dough for bread when a bullet came through a wooden door into the kitchen of the house and struck her in the back, killing her instantly. She had a picture of Jack Skelly in her apron pocket. She was buried in her sister's garden the following day, and her mother baked 15 loaves of bread with the dough Ginnie had kneaded.

She never got Jack Skelly's message, nor the news that he died nine days later on July 12 from his wounds. The two passed away without knowing the other's fate.

In January 1864, her body was relocated to the cemetery of the German Reformed Church on Stratton Street and in November 1865 again relocated to the Evergreen Cemetery in close proximity to Jack Skelly.

Wesley Culp's commanding officer sent his orderly to Culp's sister's to notify them where to find his body. Some say he was never found but his gun with his name carved in the stock was located. Others say that being a Confederate, he was secretly buried in Evergreen Cemetery. There are also those who believe he was buried in the cellar of the Culp Farm House.

Ginnie Wade was the only civilian killed directly during the battle of Gettysburg. An elaborate monument marks her grave including an American flag which flies around the clock. The only other site devoted to a woman that shares the distinction of the perpetual flag is that of The Betsy Ross House in Philadelphia.

In 1996, a book about Ginnie Wade was published. It is written by Cindy Small and called "The Jennie Wade Story." You might notice the different spelling of Ms. Wade's name. Although Cindy Small used the "Jennie" and so does the Jennie Wade House in Gettysburg, the research we did says it is unlikely anyone ever called her Jennie. Here middle name was Virginia, and she was known as Ginnie. A newspaper account of her story shortly after the battle used the name "Jennie", and it spread all over the country.

The only civilian killed during the Battle of Gettysburg.

If You Go:

Gettysburg is a history buff's paradise. The Evergreen Cemetery also contains many historic and interesting graves including John Burns (see Chapter 4) and Major League Baseball Hall of Famer Eddie Plank (See Volume II). Other graves of interest include James Gettys, the founder of Gettysburg and a soldier in the Pennsylvania Militia during the Revolution. His wife Mary Todd was an ancestor of Mary Todd Lincoln.

Elizabeth Thorn was the caretaker of Evergreen Cemetery during the Civil War. Her husband Peter enlisted in the 138th Pennsylvania and left her to care for the cemetery. She averaged five burials a month until the Battle of Gettysburg. At the time she was six months pregnant, and her duties became overwhelming. A memorial at the gatehouse depicts a pregnant Elizabeth attending her duties.

Stephen Courson, a former Pittsburgh Steeler who played in two Super Bowl Championship games and authored "False Glory" in 1991, was also laid to rest here. The book tells of steroid use in the NFL.

Also in Gettysburg is the famous Battlefield, the National Cemetery (we mention some interesting graves there in the chapter on John Burns), the Eisenhower Farm, and the Jennie Wade house among other historical sites. The Jennie Wade House is the site of her tragic death on Baltimore Street. The House is marked by over 150 bullet holes and damage caused by an artillery shell.

The Gettysburg Hotel was established in 1797 and is located across the street from the historic Will's House where President Lincoln stayed and finished the Gettysburg Address. It offers shelter at a reasonable price and contains McClelland's Tavern, a good place to obtain nourishment and replenish your fluids. The Dobbin House Tavern (est. 1776) which has a secret "underground railroad" slave hideout is another place where the authors have taken some comfort. The Farnsworth House offers Ghost Tours and a bookstore with many publications of local interest. We also stopped for a pint at O'Rorkes Eatery and Spirits on Steinwehr Avenue.

Jennie Wade's fiance' who died fighting for the Union.

Andy Warhol

29.
"The Pope of Pop"

Andy Warhol
County: Allegheny
Town: Bethel Park
Cemetery: Saint John the Baptist Byzantine
Catholic Cemetery
Address: Intersection of Connor Road and State
Route 88

He was known as the "Pope of Pop." He was famous worldwide as a painter, filmmaker, record producer, and author. He was the first to come up with the phrase "fifteen minutes of fame." He was also well known because of the people with whom he associated. These groups included intellectuals, celebrities, the very wealthy, and street people living a Bohemian life style. He is buried in Pennsylvania, about five miles outside of his hometown of Pittsburgh.

Andy Warhol was born and named Andy Warhola on August 6, 1928. Warhol's father immigrated to the United States from Slovakia in 1914. His mother arrived in the States in 1921. Warhol's father found employment in a coal mine. Warhol had two older brothers and the family attended a Byzantine Catholic Church.

At an early age, Warhol exhibited talent in drawing and painting. However, he was not a healthy child. He was often bed-ridden, and he had few friends at school. Because of the time he spent at home, his relationship with his mother was a close one. On days when he couldn't make it to school, he passed the time listening to the radio. During this period, he also began collecting pictures of movie stars. Warhol would come to believe that this period in his life was very important in developing his personality. When he was thirteen, his father was killed in a work accident.

After he graduated from high school, Warhol studied commercial art at the Carnegie Institute of Technology in Pittsburgh. He graduated in 1949 and found employment in New York City doing magazine illustrations and advertising. The magazines he worked for included "Vogue" and "Harper's Bazaar". He quickly became one of the most sought after commercial artists in New York City.

It was in the fifties that Warhol began exhibiting his own work. His New York shows were met with much success. By the early 1960's, he was ready to take his work across the country to the west coast. On July 9, 1962, he opened an exhibition in Los Angeles that marked the premiere of his pop art out west. Later in that same year he opened another exhibit in New York City. This show included the works titled "Marilyn Diptych", "100 Soup Cans", and "100 Coke Bottles." It was during this time that Andy began to paint celebrities such as Marilyn Monroe, Elvis, and Muhammad Ali. He also founded "The Factory," the studio that became the center of his work. Other artists, musicians, and underground celebrity types were drawn to him. His work while popular was controversial.

In December of 1962, New York's Museum of Modern Art held a conference on pop art. Warhol was attacked for surrendering to consumerism. Such attacks on Warhol and his work became common during the sixties. Warhol was changing the way people viewed art. In fact he was raising the question "What is and what isn't art?" As the leader of the pop movement, he became an inviting target to critics.

It was during this time that Warhol branched out into filmmaking. He made more than 60 films between 1963 and 1968. Warhol discovered his own stars for his films and named them superstars. This group included Edie Sedgwick, Jackie Curtis, Nico, Viva, and Ultra Violet among others. An emerging young singer by the name of Bob Dylan did screen tests for Warhol. There is speculation that Dylan's relationship with Edie Sedgwick ended any chance of Dylan and Warhol working together. Why this proved a strain is anybody's guess as Warhol was a homosexual. The films themselves were often unusual. For example the movie "Sleep" monitors a sleeping man for six hours. Another film titled "Empire" is eight hours long and treats the viewer to scenes of the Empire State Building at dusk. His most successful film was "Chelsea Girls" which was released in 1966. His last film was 1968's "Blue Movie," which stars Viva, shows the star having sex and fooling around in bed with a man for about 33 minutes. In the seventies, Warhol pulled the films he had directed out of circulation. After his death, some of the films were restored and are shown occasionally at film festivals.

On June 3, 1968 a woman, Valerie Solanas, showed up at the Factory and attempted to retrieve a script she had given to Warhol. When the script couldn't be located, she was turned away. Solanas was known at the Factory, having appeared in Warhol's 1968 film "I, A Man." Later that day, Solanas returned to Warhol's studio and shot him and art critic Mario Amaya. While Amaya received only minor injuries, Warhol was seriously wounded. Surgeons had to open his chest and massage his heart to save him. Solanas was arrested the next day. She said she shot Warhol because he had too much control over her life. He would suffer physical effects from the shooting until the day he died and the incident also had an effect on his art. News coverage of the assault ended quickly when Senator Robert F. Kennedy was assassinated two days later.

Compared to the turbulent sixties, Warhol's life aroused much less controversy in the following decade. During the seventies, Warhol worked at lining up the rich and famous for portrait commissions. His clients included the Shah of Iran, John Lennon, Diana Ross, and Mick Jagger. In 1975, he published the book "The Philosophy of Andy Warhol." One of the ideas he sets forth in the book is "Making money is art, and working is art and good business is the best art." During this period Warhol could be found at high profile New York nightspots including the famous Studio 54. Those who observed him described him as quiet and shy.

In the eighties, Warhol aligned himself with young and upcoming artists. Partially due to this, he had a re-emergence in terms of critical and financial success. By this time, the critics were calling Warhol a "business artist," and they didn't mean it in a good way. The critics jumped on his seventies portraits of celebrities describing them as commercial and without any depth. Since then, other art critics have come to admire the images calling them, among other things, a brilliant mirror of those times. Warhol, who always had a special place in his heart for Hollywood, summed it up himself by saying, "I love Los Angeles. I love Hollywood. They're so beautiful. Everything's plastic, but I love plastic. I want to be plastic."

In February of 1987, Warhol entered a New York hospital for routine gallbladder surgery. By all reports, the surgery was a success and he was on the road to recovery. However, at around 6:30 in the morning on February 22, 1987, Warhol died in his sleep. The cause of death was a sudden cardiac arrhythmia.

Warhol's brothers arranged to have his body returned to Pittsburgh for burial. In the coffin Warhol was dressed in a black suit, a paisley tie, a platinum wig, and he was wearing sunglasses. Yoko Ono made an appearance at the service. At the conclusion of the Mass, Warhol's body was taken to Saint John the Baptist Byzantine Catholic Cemetery in Bethel Park. Warhol was laid to rest next to his mother and father. However, before the coffin was lowered into the grave, a bottle of Estee Lauder perfume called "Beautiful" was laid beneath him. New York City didn't forget Andy. On April 1, 1987 a memorial service was held at Saint Patrick's Cathedral. More than 20,000 people attended.

If You Go:

The cemetery is divided into two levels. Warhol is buried on the upper half approximately a quarter of the way through the cemetery from the upper entrance. The burial site is on the right side of the road and should be easy to spot. Look for Campbell soup cans.

The noted artist lies buried in the family plot outside of Pittsburgh. Note the grave goods left by visitors, these includes Campbell Soup Cans, coins, and a guitar pick.

There are plenty of things to do and see in Pittsburgh, but if you make this trip you may want to visit the Andy Warhol Museum located on the north side of the city at 117 Sandusky Street. While you are on the north side, should you be in need of refreshment, we made a stop at a nearby spot called "The Tilted Kilt." The establishment features a very attractive work staff who provide excellent service.

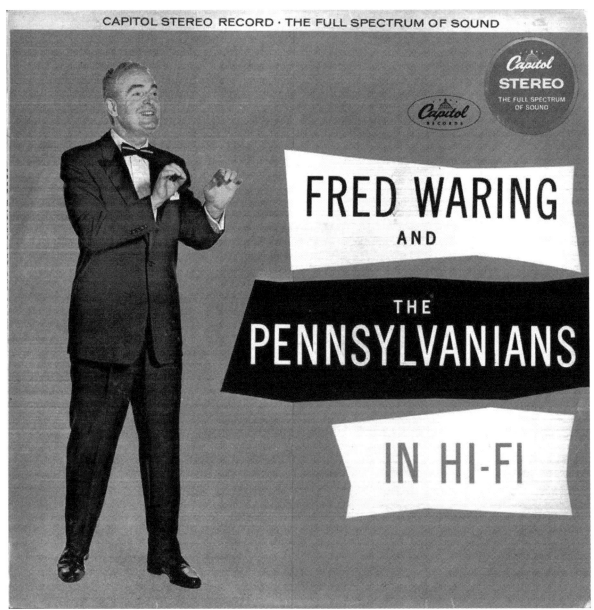

Fred Waring and the Pennsylvanians album cover.

30.
"The Man Who Taught America How To Sing"

Fred Waring and His Band the Pennsylvanians
County: Monroe
Town: Shawnee on the Delaware
Cemetery: Shawnee Presbyterian Church Cemetery
Address: None listed but anyone in the area will provide directions

Fred Waring was a popular musician, bandleader, and radio-television personality sometimes referred to as "The Man Who Taught America How to Sing". We bet that many of you thought that honor belonged to Mitch Miller. Waring was also the promoter and financial backer of the Waring Blendor, the first modern electric blender.

Fredric Malcolm Waring was born June 9, 1900 in Tyrone Pennsylvania. As a teenager, he formed what became known as Waring's Banjo Orchestra. The band played at fraternity parties, proms, and dances and achieved local success. He attended Penn State University where he studied architectural engineering. He wanted badly to become a member of the Penn State Glee Club but was rejected after auditioning. Waring's Banjo Orchestra became so popular he decided to leave college in order to pursue touring with his band. As it turned out, in Waring's case, leaving the educational world behind proved to be a good move. It appears the entertainment world was ready for his style of music. Waring initially named his band The Pennsylvanians, and they recorded a tune for Thomas Edison called "Sleep". It became their first theme song. The band continued to grow and soon became known as Fred Waring and the Pennsylvanians. From 1923 until 1932, they were among Victor Records best selling bands. In the 1930's, Waring's band had grown to 55 pieces and attained a six month booking at the famous Roxy Theater in New York City along with its very own radio program.

Aside from music, Waring was a talented innovator and businessman. In 1933, Fred Osius invented and patented a household blender with Waring's financial help. Waring took over the project, redesigned the blender, and launched the Waring Blendor (the "o" in blendor giving it a slight distinction). The blender became popular in the medical field. It was used in the care of patients who had special diets. In addition, the Waring Blendor was utilized by those doing medical research. As a matter of fact,

Jonas Salk used it in his development of the polio vaccine. In the mid-fifties, the millionth Waring blendor was sold. It remains a popular item to this day.

During World War II, Waring and his ensemble appeared at war bond rallies and entertained the troops at training camps. He composed and performed many patriotic songs. The most famous of these compositions was "My America." In 1943, he acquired the Buckwood Inn in Shawnee of Delaware Pennsylvania, renamed it the Shawnee Inn, and made it the center of his musical activities. He created, rehearsed, and broadcast his radio programs from the Shawnee Inn. In doing so, he was able to advertise and successfully market the property.

The year 1943 was a big one for Waring as he also decided to launch his own music publishing company. He called it Words and Music, but later changed it to Shawnee Press. Waring's publishing company soon became one of the largest and most successful in terms of the publishing and sale of choral music. He even formed a male chorus apart from the Pennsylvanians. His approach to choral singing was embraced by the nation. Up until the day he died, he taught and supervised workshops on the subject of choral singing.

During the 1940's and early 50's, Waring and his Pennsylvanians produced a string of hits and sold millions of records. Some of his biggest hits were "You Gotta be a Football Hero", "Button Up Your Overcoat", "Sleep", and "Dancing in the Dark". Waring and the Pennsylvanians grew so popular that in addition to his radio show he moved into television. In June of 1948, "The Fred Waring Show" premiered on CBS. It would run until 1954 and receive multiple awards for Best Musical Program.

Waring also knew it was important to change with the times. In the 1960's as American's tastes in popular music changed, he adapted as well. He formed a group called the Young Pennsylvanians. Members followed the fashions of the times wearing bellbottoms and growing long hair. They performed choral arrangements of currently popular songs. They toured the country and were a popular attraction.

Waring was a big fan of cartoon and comic strips. After being featured in a New York Herald Tribune strip, he invited members of the National Cartoonists Society to the Shawnee Inn as his guests. The artists loved it. Waring would hire buses to provide for their transportation and when they arrived at the Shawnee, all was taken care of. As one of the cartoonists remarked, "he [Fred] had it all." The outing became an annual event held each June for the next 25 years. It resulted in a huge collection of artwork created for Waring by the cartoonists, many of which were turned into table tops at the Shawnee Inn. If you visit the Fred Waring collection at Penn State University today, you can view some of the work. It includes over 600 cartoons and more than 50 of the laminated table tops.

Throughout his life, Waring received plenty of recognition for his musical work, inventions and devotion to the public. He is commemorated by a star at 6556 Hollywood Boulevard on the Hollywood Walk of Fame. Perhaps the most prestigious award was the Congressional Gold Medal he received in 1983 from President Ronald Reagan.

A year after receiving this great award, Fred Waring died on July 29, 1984 after complications following a massive stroke. He was 84 years of age. He had come full circle as the place of his death was Penn State University. He had just completed a workshop on choral singing.

Shortly before he died, Waring designated Penn State to house his collection of archives. The Fred Waring Collection, known as Fred Waring's America, contains the historical memorabilia, music library, recordings, scrapbooks, photographs, cartoons, and business and personal correspondence that reflect his nearly 70 year career as a choral conductor, showman, and pioneer of show business.

If You Go:

Shawnee on Delaware is a charming town and the Shawnee Inn is still a thriving, picturesque resort. The area is filled with attractions that include live entertainment, skiing, and white water rafting depending on the season. We had lunch at nearby Alaska Pete's Roadhouse Grille and Moondog Saloon on Route 209. The sandwiches were big and tasty and the service was friendly and attentive. It's a stop we would both recommend.

Fred Waring lies here without the Pennsylvanians, though no real Pennsylvanian will ever forget his contributions in both the entertainment field and household appliances.

181

UNUSUAL TOMBSTONES

This unusual monument honors the Philadelphia writer Charles Brown.

The Brown pyramid in Pittsburgh.

Monument in Pittsburgh erected by the Woodmen of the World to honor one of their own.

He must have loved to ski.

Here lies a man who would have loved the Chapter titled Half the Horsemen that appears in this volume.

Index

Congressional Medal of Honor Recipients

Cemeteries

Cities and Towns

Pubs and Restaurants

June
2013

Made in the USA
Charleston, SC
30 May 2013